Differentiation Pack 1

Series Editor: Peter Clarke

Authors: Jo Power-O'Keeffe, Andrew Edmondson

William Collins' dream of knowledge for all began with the publication of his first book in 1819. A self-educated mill worker, he not only enriched millions of lives, but also founded a flourishing publishing house. Today, staying true to this spirit, Collins books are packed with inspiration, innovation and practical expertise. They place you at the centre of a world of possibility and give you exactly what you need to explore it.

Collins. Freedom to teach.

Published by Collins
An imprint of HarperCollinsPublishers
77 – 85 Fulham Palace Road
Hammersmith
London
W6 8JB

Browse the complete Collins catalogue at
www.collinseducation.com

10 9 8 7 6 5

ISBN-13 978-00-0-722010-6

British Library Cataloguing in Publication Data
A Catalogue record for this publication is available from the British Library

Cover design by Laing&Carroll
Cover artwork by Jonatronix Ltd
Internal design by Mark Walker and Steve Evans Design
Illustrations by Mark Walker and Steve Evans
Edited by Jean Rustean
Proofread by Amanda Dickson

Printed and bound by Martins the Printers, Berwick-upon-Tweed

Mixed Sources
Product group from well-managed
forests and other controlled sources
www.fsc.org Cert no. SW-COC-1806
© 1996 Forest Stewardship Council

FSC

FSC is a non-profit international organisation established to promote the responsible management of the world's forests. Products carrying the FSC label are independently certified to assure consumers that they come from forests that are managed to meet the social, economic and ecological needs of present and future generations.

Find out more about HarperCollins and the environment at
www.harpercollins.co.uk/green

Contents

Contents

Contents

Unit A3

Unit B3

Unit C3

Contents

Name _____ Date _____

Missing numbers

- **Read and write numbers from 0 to 10**

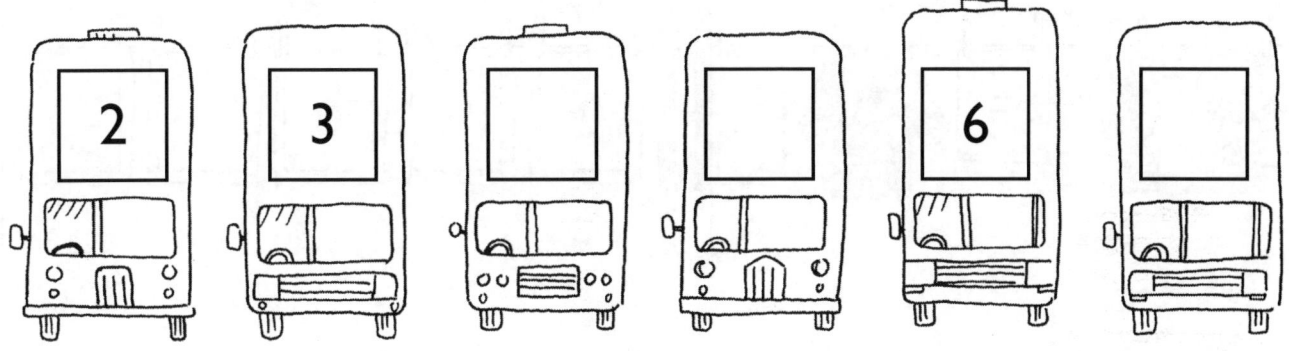

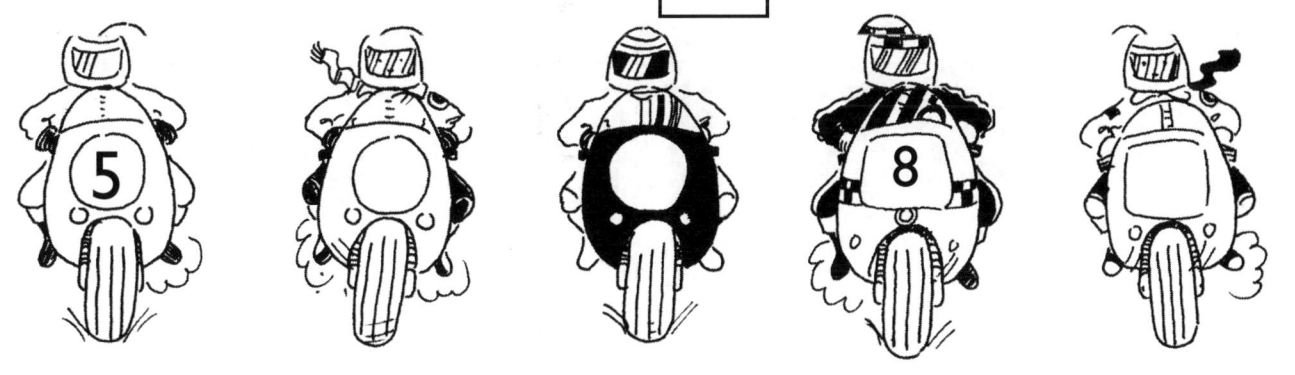

Teacher's notes
Complete each number sequence by writing numbers in the spaces.

Name _____ Date _____

Washing line addition

● Write addition number sentences

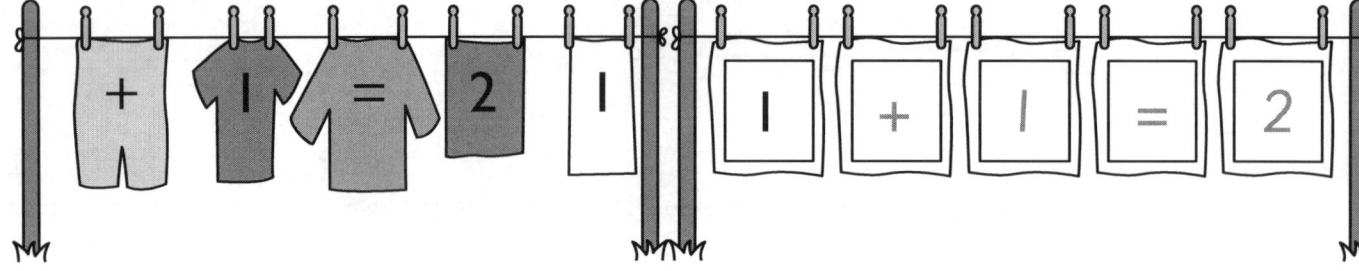

`+` `1` `=` `2` `1` | `1` `+` `1` `=` `2`

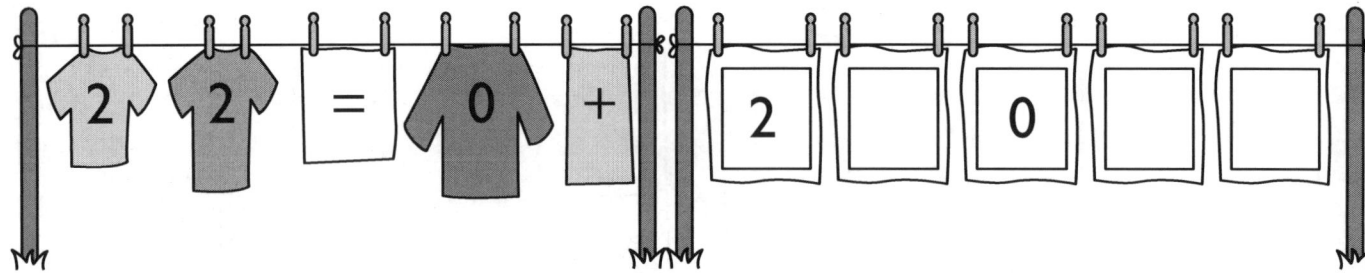

`2` `2` `=` `0` `+` | `2` `0`

`=` `1` `3` `+` `2` | `1` `2`

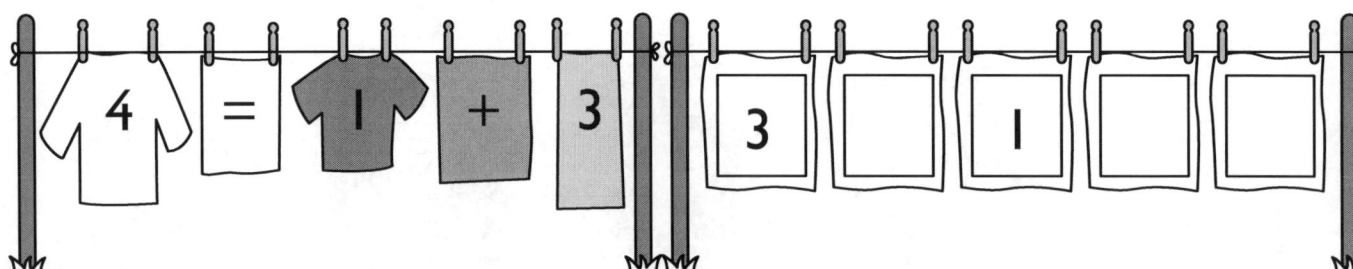

`4` `=` `1` `+` `3` | `3` `1`

`2` `+` `5` `=` `3` | `3` `2`

Teacher's notes
Look at each washing line. Unscramble the calculations on the left hand line and write them in the correct order on the right hand line.

Name _____ Date _____

Take away cubes

- **Understand subtraction as 'taking away'**

 – 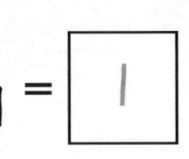 = 1

 – 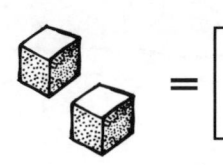 = ☐

 – 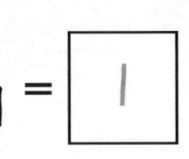 = ☐

 – 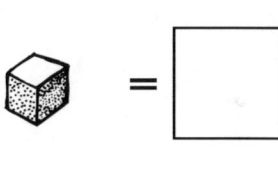 = ☐

 – 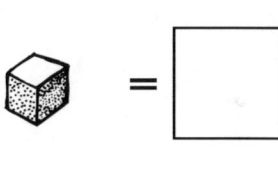 = ☐

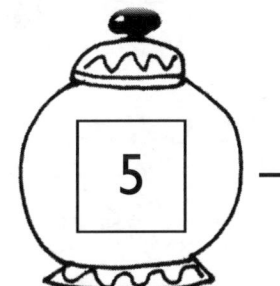 – 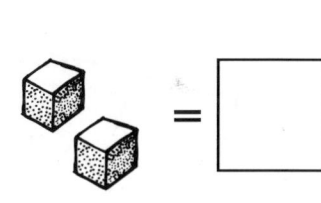 = ☐

 – 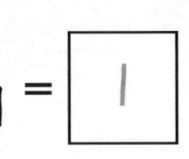 = ☐

 – 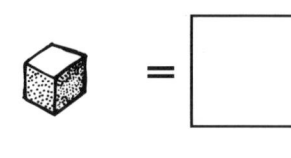 = ☐

 – 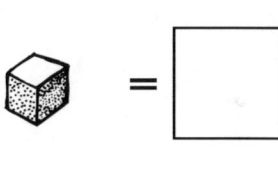 = ☐

 – 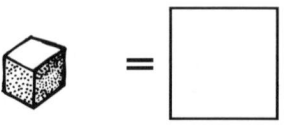 = ☐

Teacher's notes
Look at the number of cubes in each secret box. Take away the number of cubes
shown and write how many are left in the square.

Name _____ Date _____

Money bags

You need:
● scissors ● glue

● **Solve problems using money**

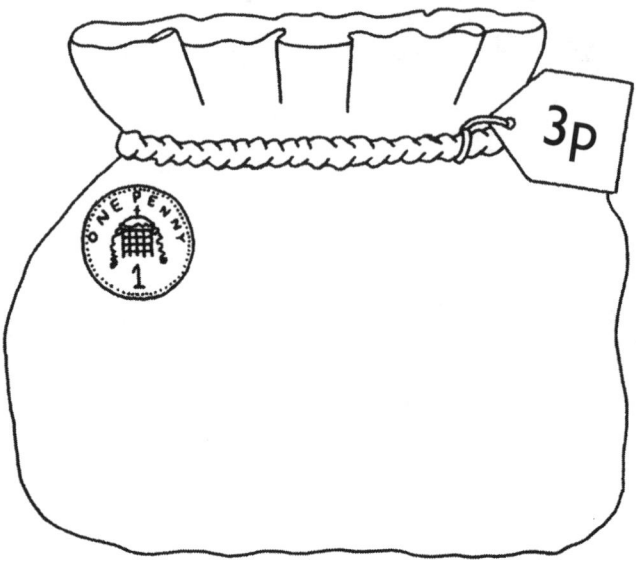

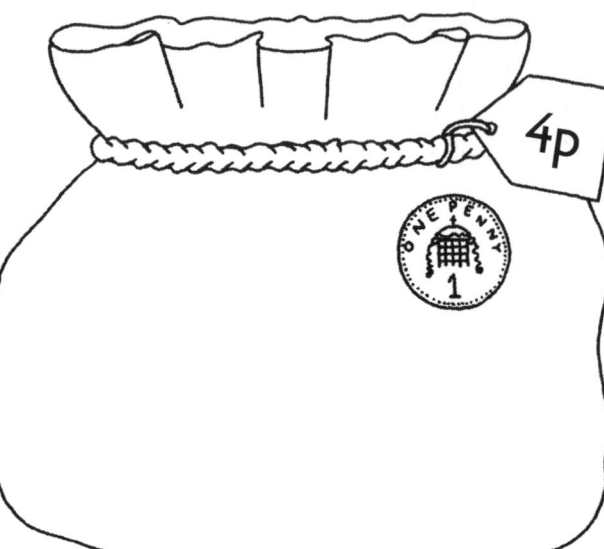

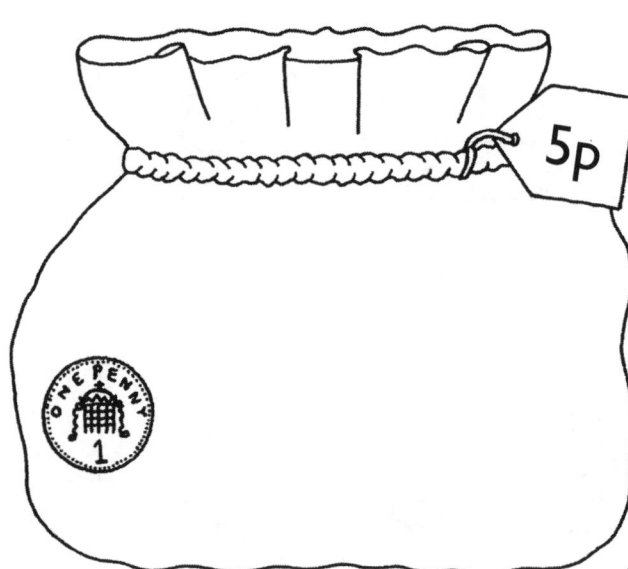

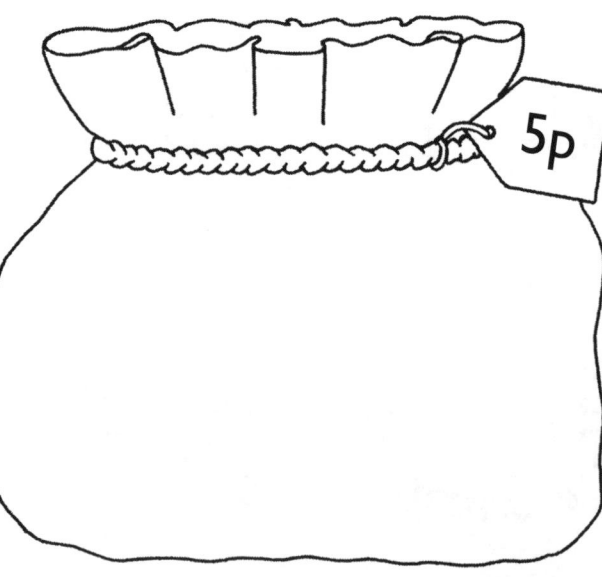

Teacher's notes
Cut out the coins from the bottom of the sheet and share them amongst the money bags, so that the total in each is the amount shown on the label. When all the coins have been sorted correctly, stick them on to the money bags.

Name _____ Date _____

One more or less

● **Work out the number that is 1 more or less**

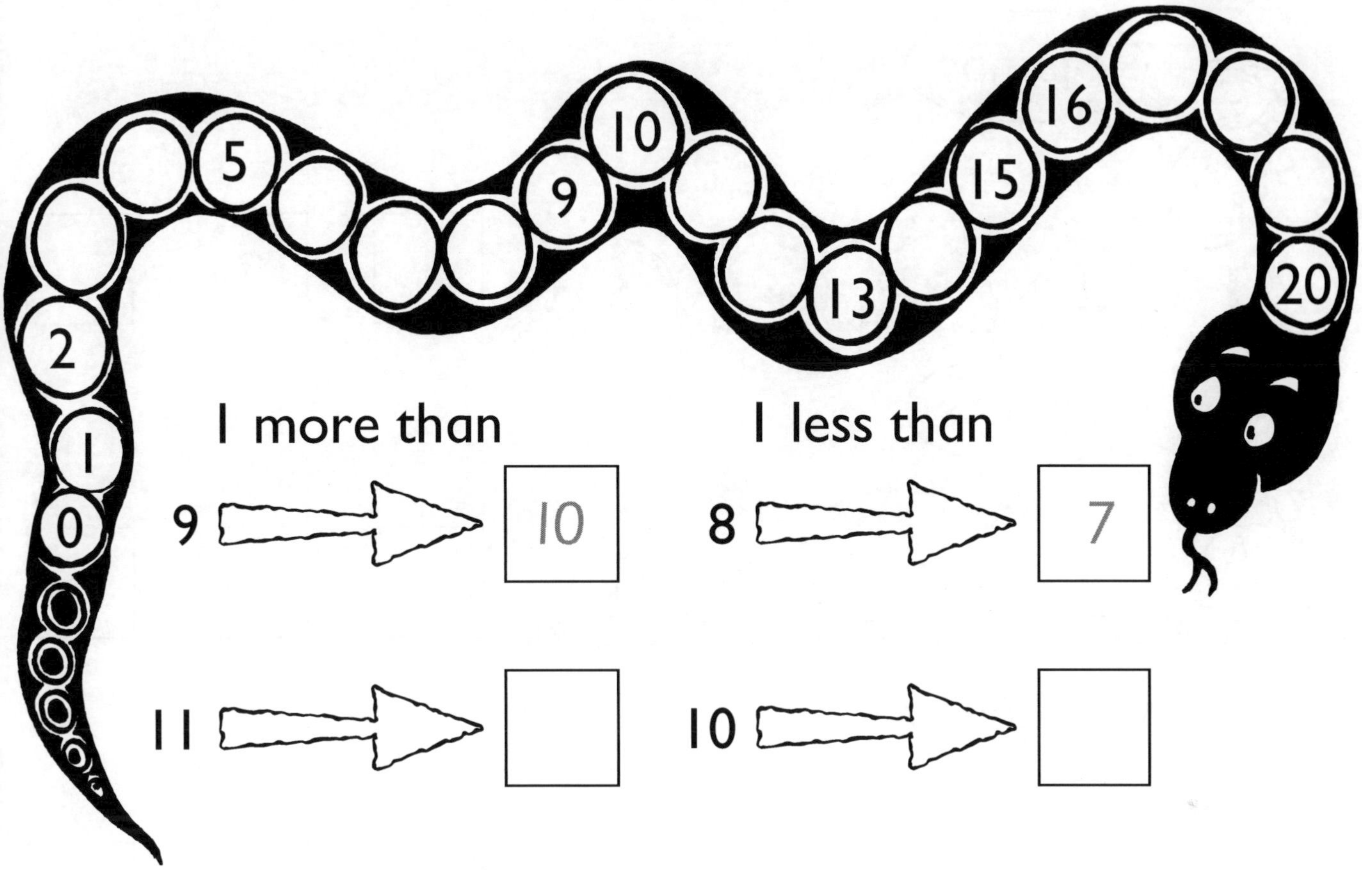

I more than   I less than

9 ➡️ $\boxed{10}$ 8 ➡️ $\boxed{7}$

11 ➡️ ☐   10 ➡️ ☐

14 ➡️ ☐   13 ➡️ ☐

15 ➡️ ☐   15 ➡️ ☐

17 ➡️ ☐   17 ➡️ ☐

19 ➡️ ☐   19 ➡️ ☐

Snake numbers: 2 1 0 5 9 10 13 15 16 20

Teacher's notes
Complete the number line on the snake by writing in the missing numbers.
Then use the snake number line to find one more or one less than each given number,
writing the answer in the box.

Name _____ Date _____

Adding on stepping stones

● **Add two numbers**

2 jumps

1 2 3 4 5

$\boxed{1}$ + $\boxed{2}$ = $\boxed{}$

4 jumps

1 2 3 4 5

$\boxed{}$ + $\boxed{}$ = $\boxed{}$

3 jumps

2 3 4 5 6

$\boxed{}$ + $\boxed{}$ = $\boxed{}$

3 jumps

3 4 5 6 7

$\boxed{}$ + $\boxed{}$ = $\boxed{}$

2 jumps

4 5 6 7 8

$\boxed{}$ + $\boxed{}$ = $\boxed{}$

Teacher's notes
In each row, start by writing in the first box the number on the first stone.
Then count on the number of jumps given by the character standing on the first rock.
Complete the calculation by writing the correct numbers in the other two boxes.

Name _____ Date _____

Finding the difference

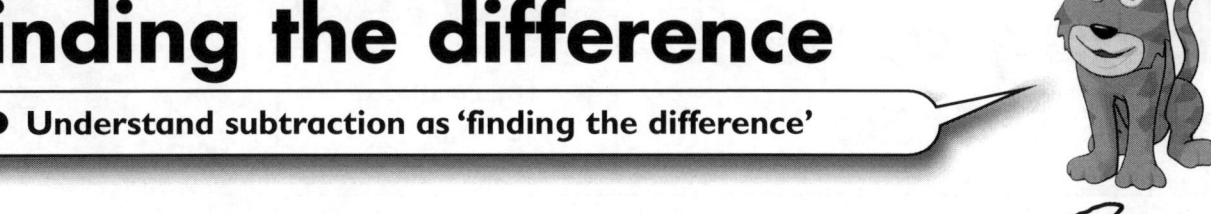

● **Understand subtraction as 'finding the difference'**

| 3 | 1 | → | 2 |

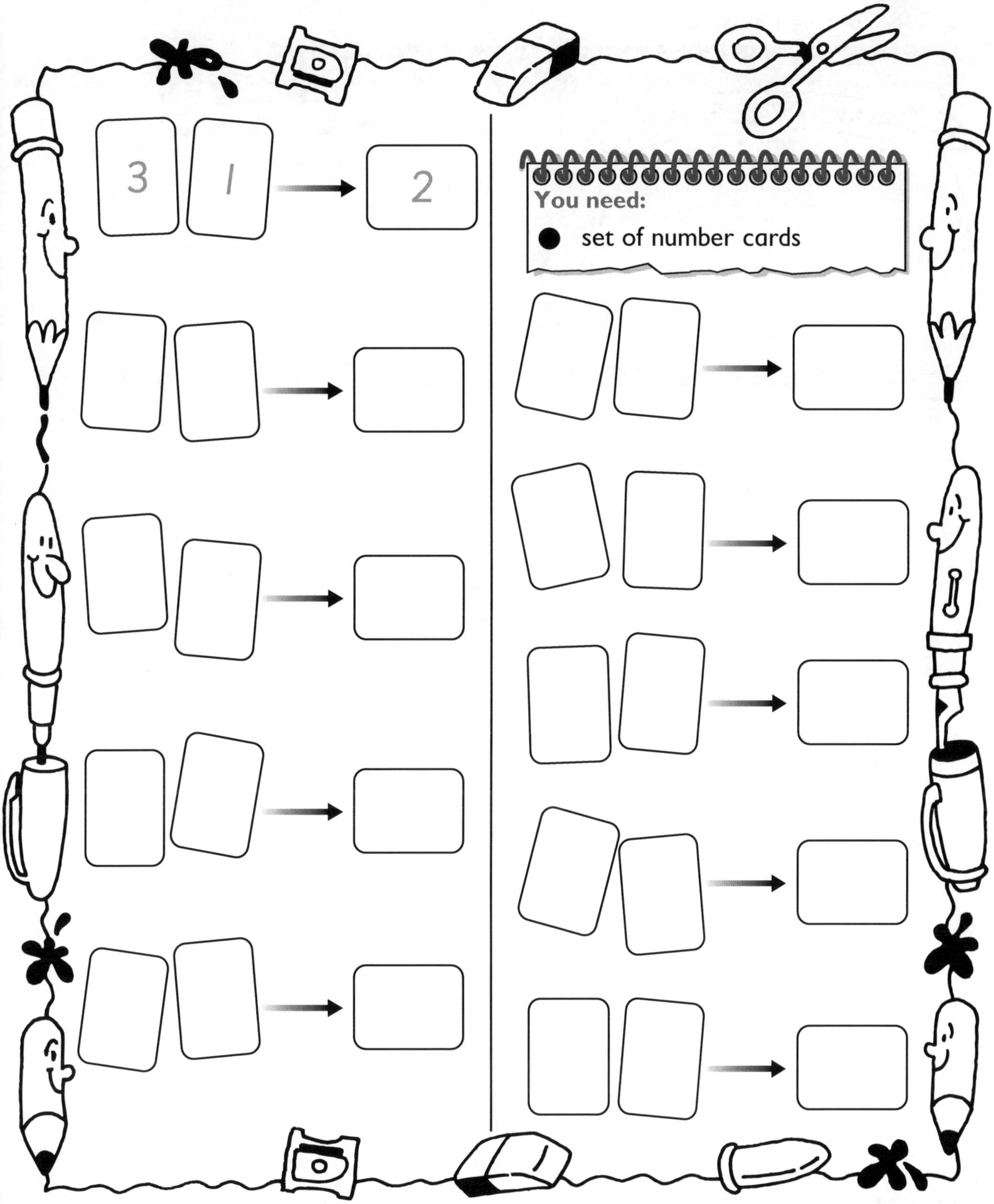

You need:

● set of number cards

Teacher's notes
Children shuffle the cards and place them face down in a pile. They then turn over the top two cards and find the difference, writing the numbers on the 'blank cards'. They do this 10 times.

Name _____ Date _____

Putting coins in your purse

You need:
- 1p, 2p and 5p coin

- Solve problems using money

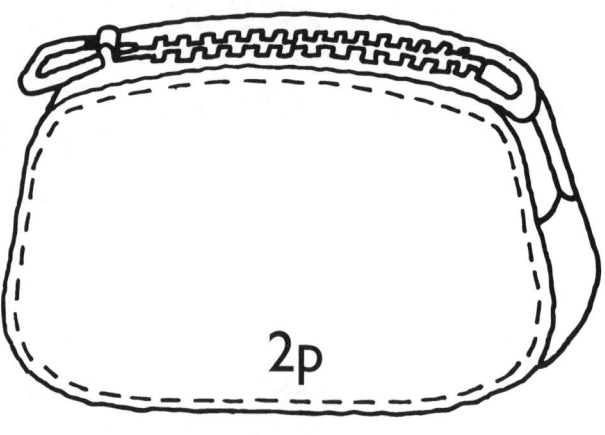

2p

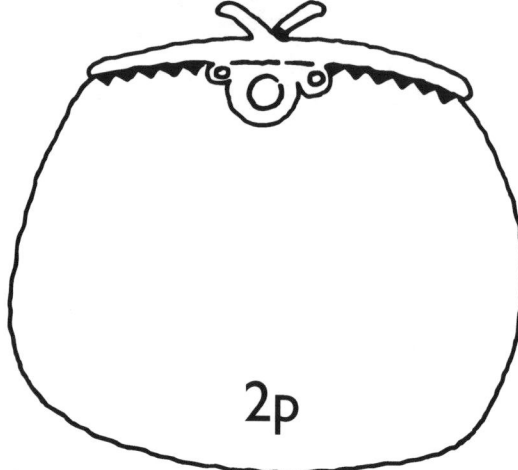

2p

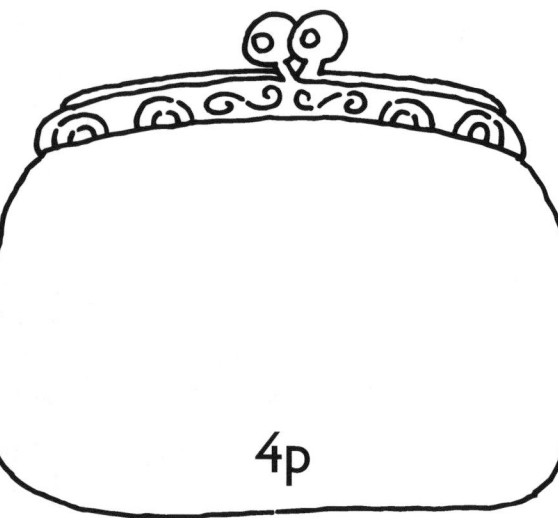

4p

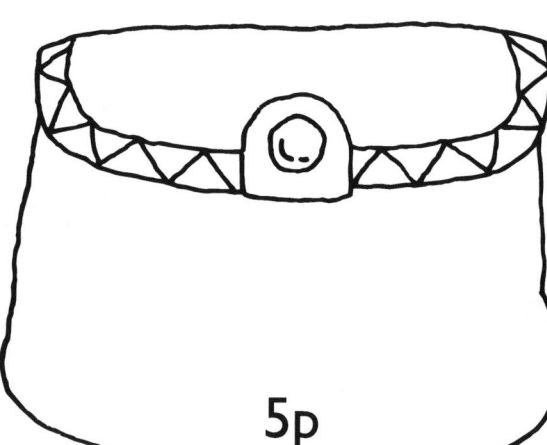

5p

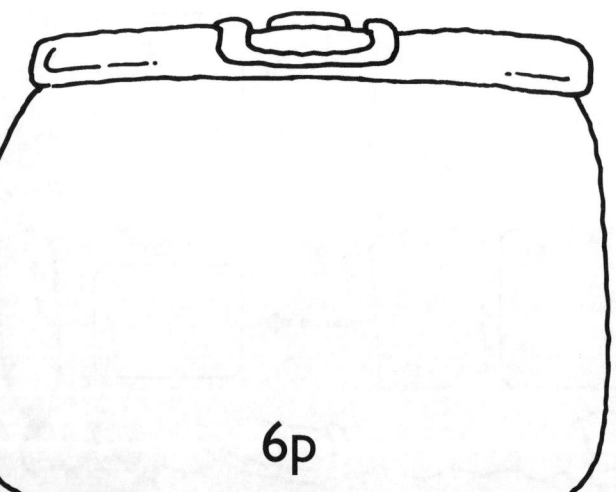

6p

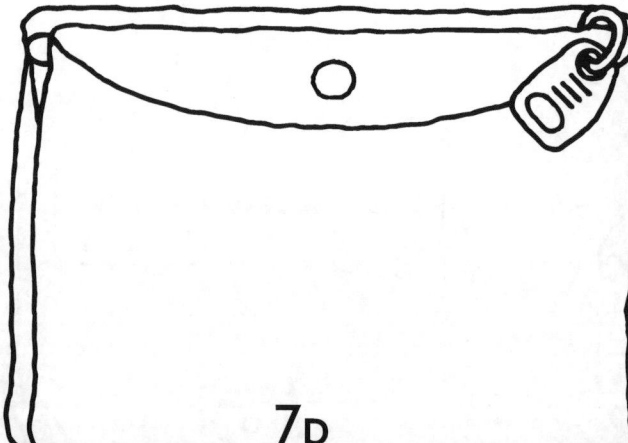

7p

Teacher's notes
Inside each purse, make rubbings of coins to the value given on the purse.

Name _____ Date _____

Adding up to five

● **Add two numbers with answers up to 5**

3 + 1 = 4

0 + 2 =

2 + 1 =

0 + 5 =

1 + 0 =

1 + 4 =

0 + 5 =

2 + 0 =

3 + 0 =

0 + 3 =

4 + 0 =

1 + 2 =

0 + 4 =

2 + 2 =

4 + 1 =

3 + 2 =

5 + 0 =

2 + 3 =

0 + 1 =

1 + 3 =

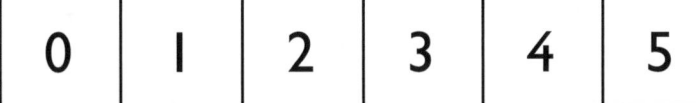

0	1	2	3	4	5

Teacher's notes
Write the answers to the calculations in the boxes. If necessary, children use the
0–5 number track at the bottom of the sheet to help them.

Name _____ Date _____

Making cakes, taking cakes

You need:
- scissors
- glue

● **Add and subtract numbers**

$\boxed{2}$ + $\boxed{1}$ = $\boxed{3}$

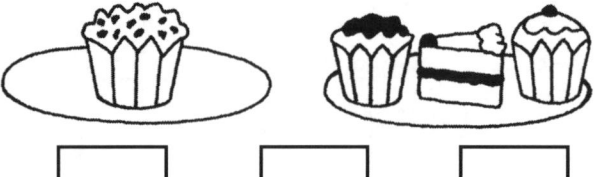 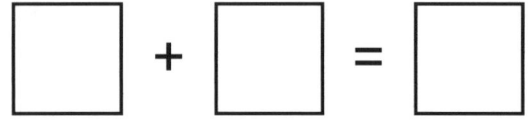 

$\boxed{}$ + $\boxed{}$ = $\boxed{}$

$\boxed{}$ + $\boxed{}$ = $\boxed{}$

$\boxed{}$ + $\boxed{}$ = $\boxed{}$

$\boxed{5}$ − $\boxed{1}$ = $\boxed{4}$ $\boxed{3}$ − $\boxed{1}$ = $\boxed{2}$

$\boxed{4}$ − $\boxed{3}$ = $\boxed{1}$ $\boxed{5}$ − $\boxed{3}$ = $\boxed{2}$

Teacher's notes

Left section: Complete the addition calculations to show the total amount of cakes on each pair of plates.
Right section: Cut out the subtraction calculations from the bottom panel and match each one to the complementary addition calculation.

Name _____ Date _____

Knights of the Round Table

You need:
- scissors ● glue

● **Recognise 2-D shapes**

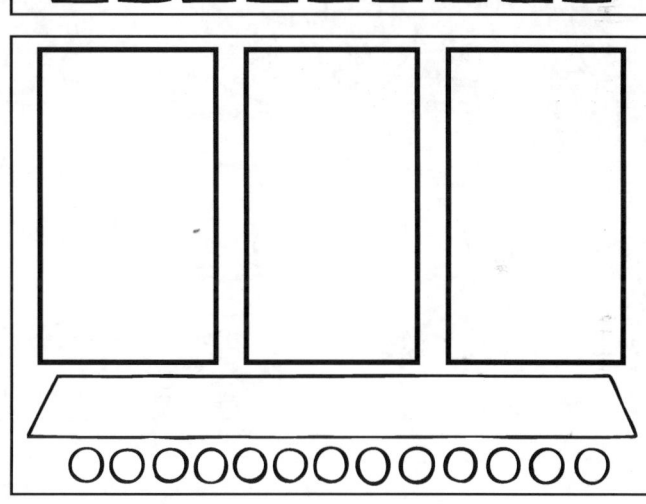

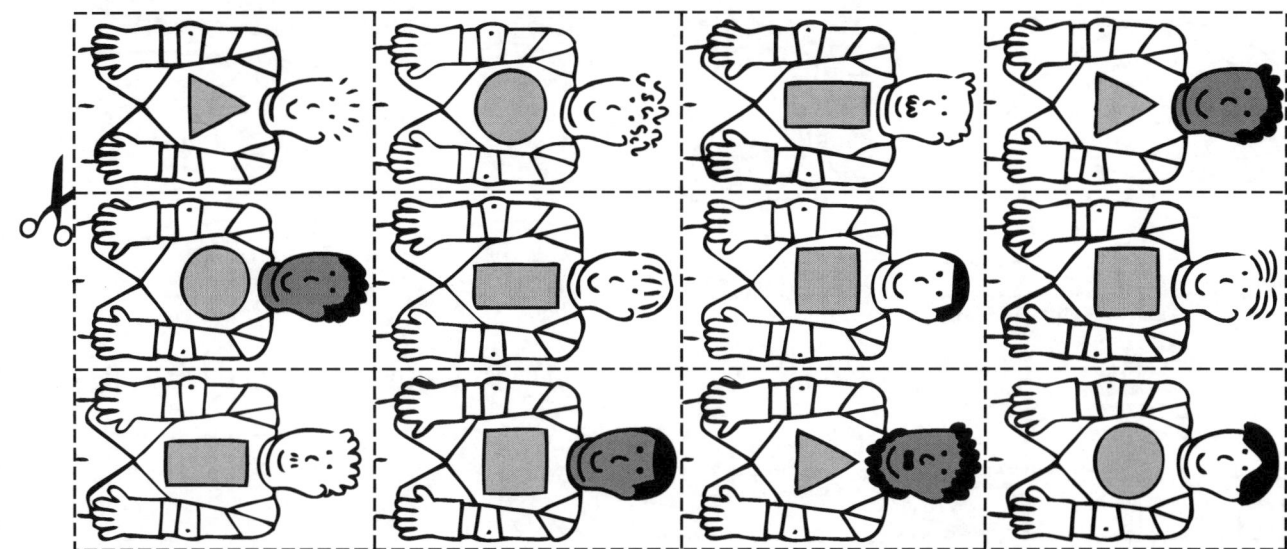

Teacher's notes
Cut out King Arthur's Knights from the bottom of the sheet and stick them onto the appropriate table, according to the shape on their armour.

Name _____ Date _____

Posting letters in order

● Order numbers to 20

Teacher's notes
Starting from 1, the post office, draw the post woman's route to her home, following the order 1-20, without doubling back or using any part of the route more than once.

Name _____ Date _____

Counting minibeasts

● **Order numbers to 20**

| 9 | 10 | 11 | 12 | 13 |

| 10 | ☐ | 12 | ☐ | 14 |

| ☐ | 13 | 14 | ☐ | ☐ | 17 |

| ☐ | 15 | ☐ | 17 |

| 15 | ☐ | 17 | ☐ | ☐ |

| 17 | ☐ | 19 | ☐ |

Teacher's notes
Complete each number sequence by writing numbers in the spaces.

Name _____ Date _____

Fruit stall number 5 and 6

- ● **Solve number puzzles**

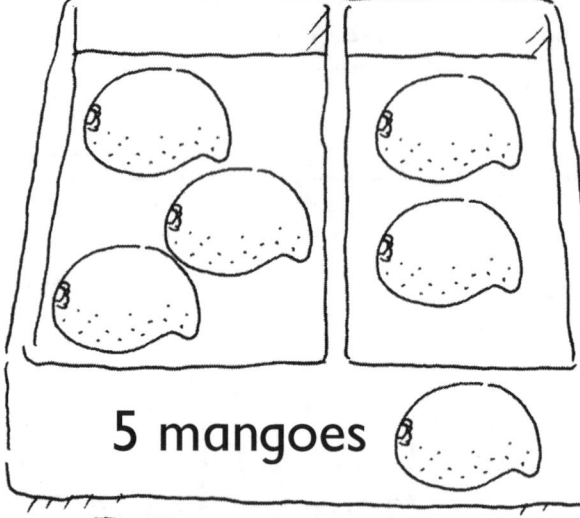

5 mangoes

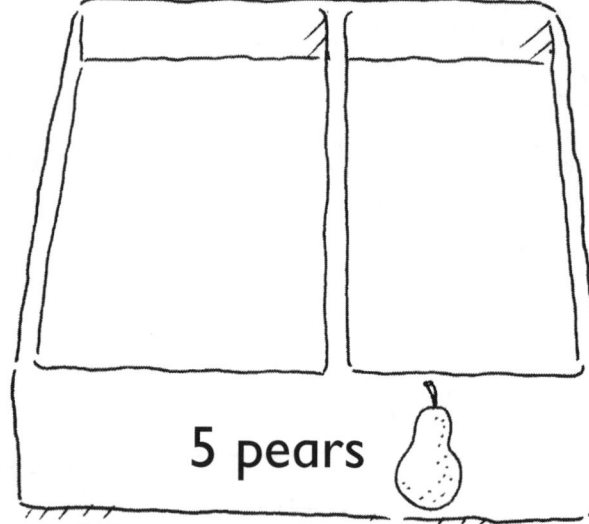

5 pears

5 bananas

6 pineapples

6 apples

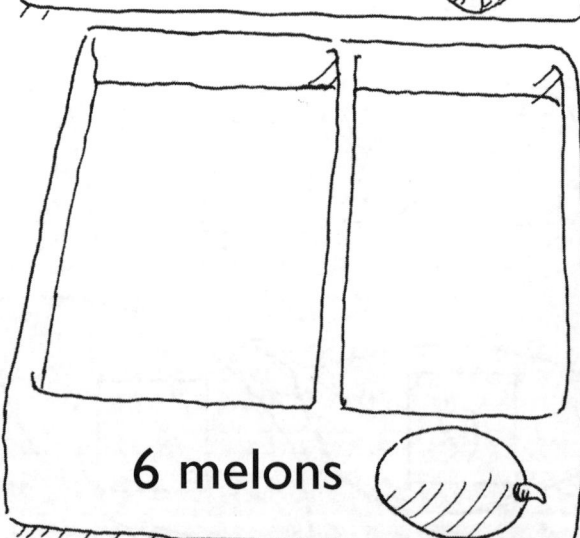

6 melons

Teacher's notes
Each crate has two compartments and holds five or six fruits. How many different ways can the fruits be arranged in the two compartments? Draw the different arrangements, using a different crate for each one.

Name _____ Date _____

Are there enough...

You need:
● colouring pencils

● **Estimate a number of objects**

... cushions for the cats?  yes (no)

Now check  4   5

Are there enough? (yes) (no)

... spoons for the bowls? 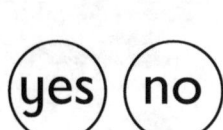 yes no

Now check 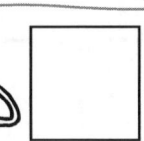 [ ]  [ ]

Are there enough? yes no

... sweets for the children? yes no

Now check  [ ]  [ ]

Are there enough? yes no

... leaves for the ladybirds? yes no

Now check  [ ] 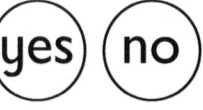 [ ]

Are there enough? yes no

Teacher's notes
For each panel, guess whether there are enough of the objects in question and then colour either the 'yes' circle or the 'no' circle. Next, check by counting both sets of objects, writing the results in the 'now check' boxes, and then colouring the appropriate decision box.

Name _____ Date _____

Acrobatic addition

You need:
- scissors
- glue
- blue coloured pencil

● Recognise that addition can be done in any order

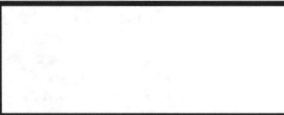

| 3 + 2 = 5 | 2 + 1 = 3 | 2 + 3 = 5 | 2 + 4 = 6 |
| 4 + 2 = 6 | 1 + 3 = 4 | 1 + 2 = 3 | 3 + 1 = 4 |

Teacher's notes
Cut out the addition calculations from the bottom of the sheet. Look at each picture and decide
which two calculations are the most appropriate. Glue them in the boxes underneath. Identify the
calculation for each set that shows the larger number first and colour this box blue.

Name _____ Date _____

The Palace of Shapes

You need:
● red, blue, yellow and green coloured pencils

● **Recognise common 2-D shapes**

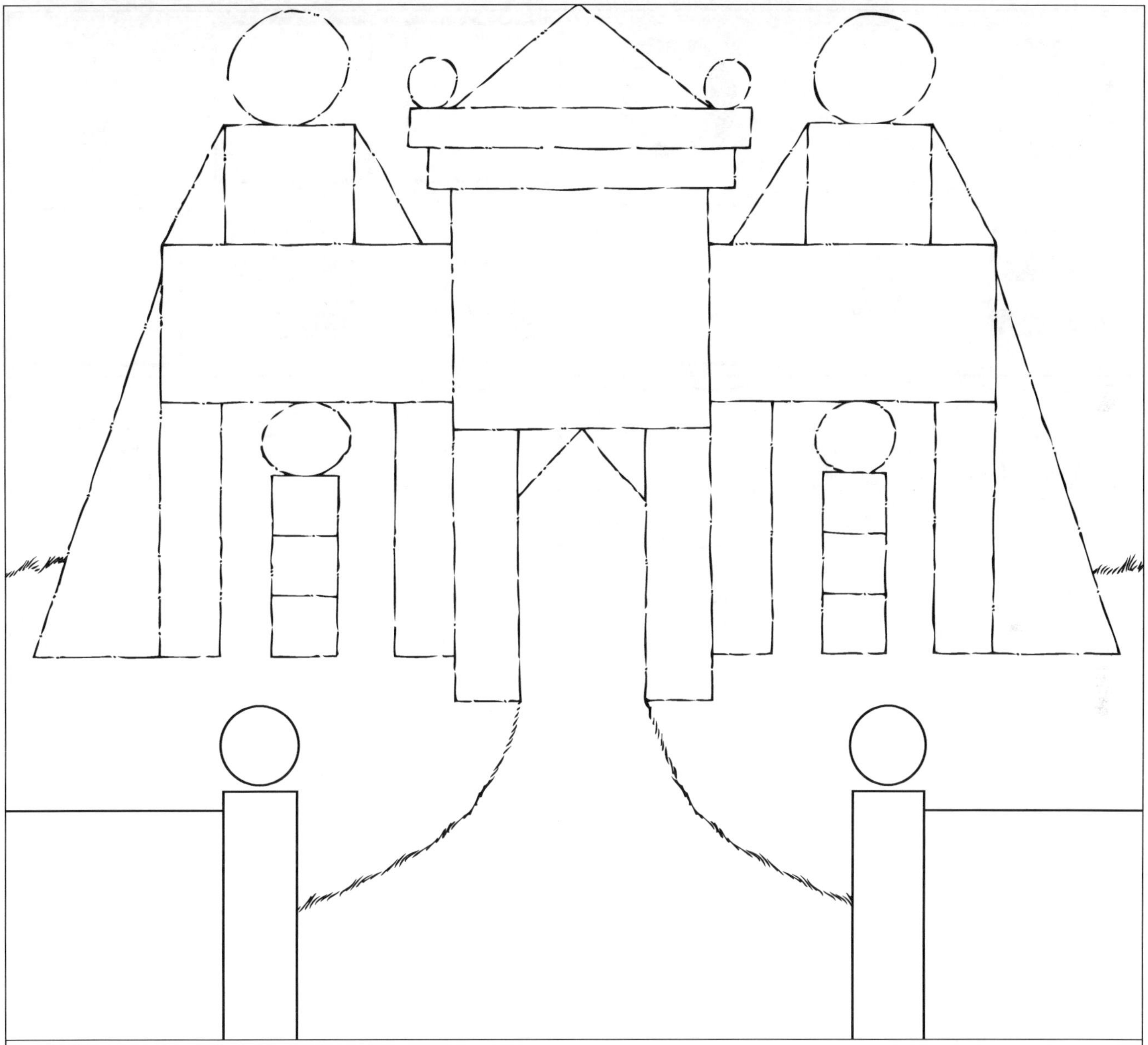

red triangles	blue circles	yellow squares	green rectangles

Teacher's notes
Colour the shapes in the palace according to the colours specified at the bottom of the sheet. Count the number of triangles, circles, squares and rectangles in the palace and write the total for each in the corresponding shapes.

Name _____ Date _____

Wallpaper patterns

You need:
- scissors
- glue

● **Use shapes to continue a simple pattern**

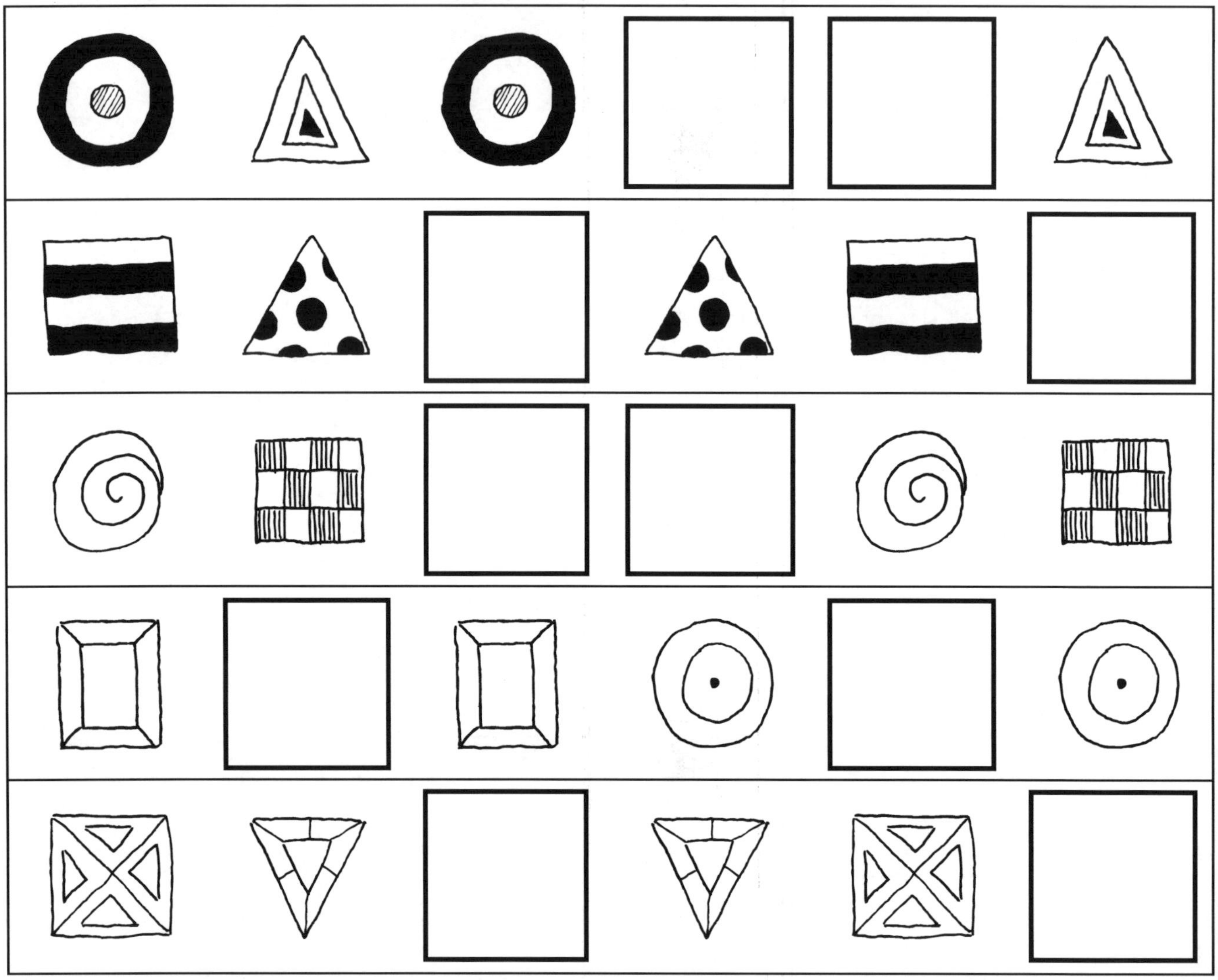

26

Teacher's notes
Cut out each of the shapes from the bottom of the sheet and stick them into the
correct places on the wallpaper borders, to complete each repeating pattern.

Name _____ Date _____

More or less apples?

● **Find the number that is 10 more or one less**

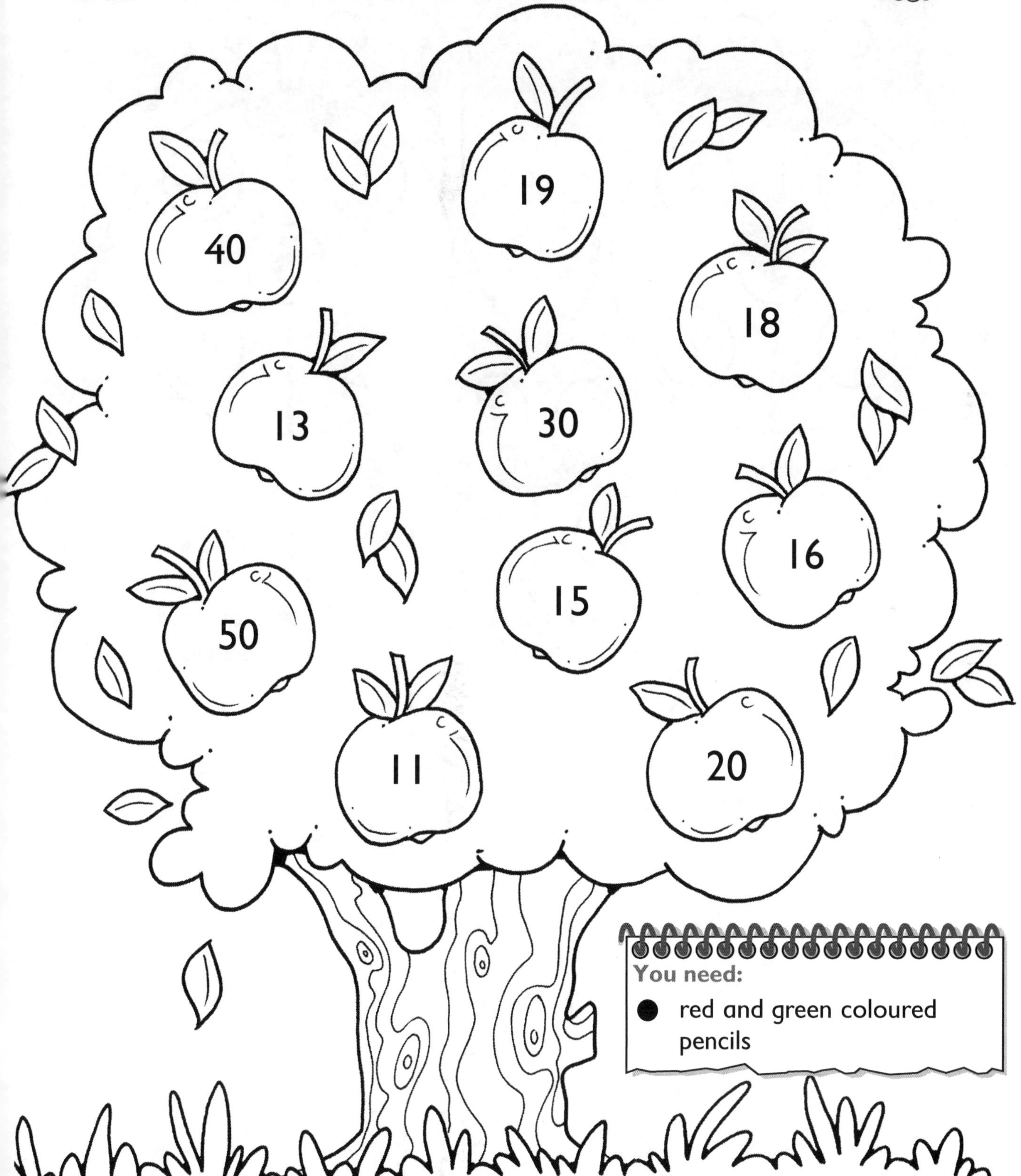

19

40

18

13

30

50

16

15

11

20

You need:

● red and green coloured pencils

© HarperCollinsPublishers Ltd 2008

Teacher's notes

Colour in red each apple whose number is 1 less than 12, 20, 14 and 17.
Colour in green each apple whose number is 10 more than 20, 40, 10 and 30.

Name _____ Date _____

Ladybird totals

● Solve a number puzzle

You need:

● coloured pencils

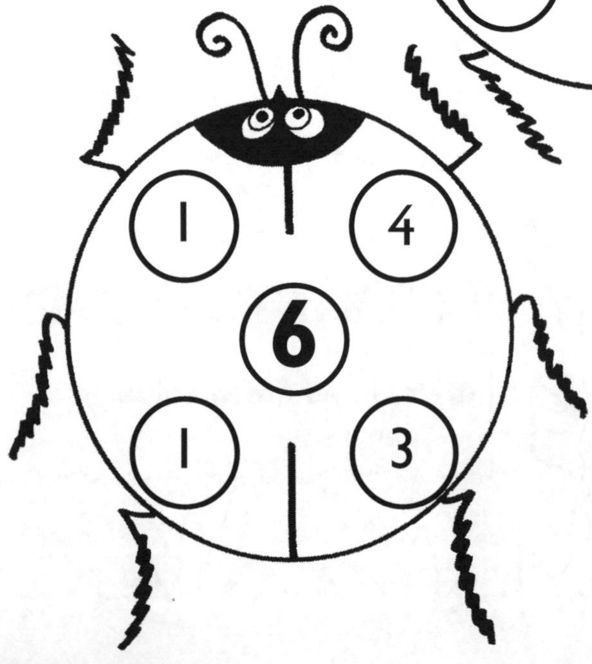

Teacher's notes

On each ladybird, identify and colour the spots whose numbers add up to the bold
number in the centre of the ladybird's back. More than two spots may be coloured.

Name _____ Date _____

Which are longer, which shorter?

You need:
● coloured pencils

● **Compare the lengths of two objects**

Teacher's notes
Top section: Colour the longer of each pair of objects.
Bottom section: Colour the shorter of each pair of objects.

29

Name _____ Date _____

Longer or shorter?

● **Estimate, measure and compare object**

These things are **longer than** a rod of 5 cubes.

These things are **shorter than** a rod of 5 cubes.

✂ -

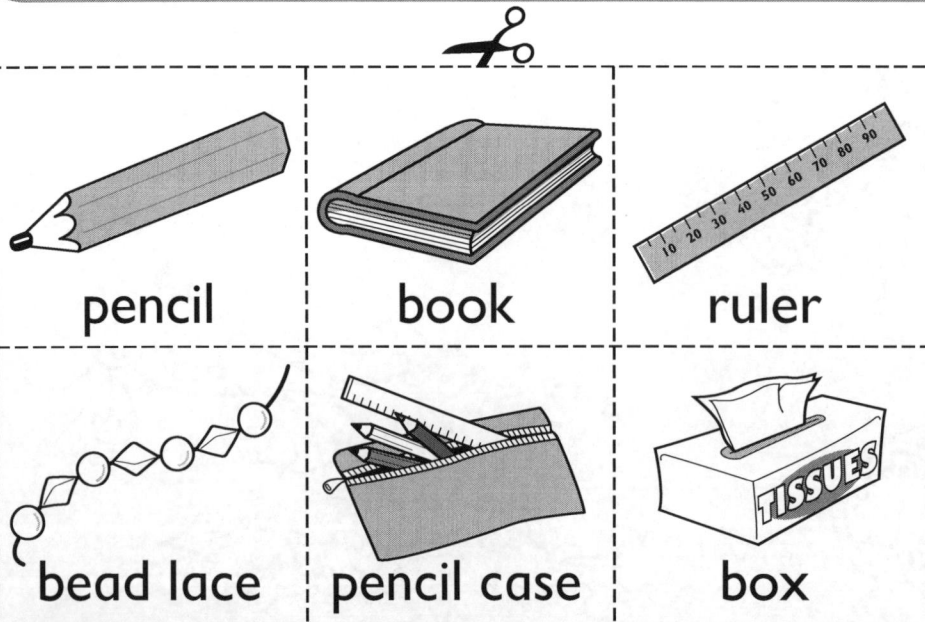

pencil	book	ruler
bead lace	pencil case	box

You need:

● 5 interlocking cubes
● pencil
● book
● ruler
● bead lace
● pencil case
● box
● scissors
● glue

Teacher's notes
Children build a rod using 5 cubes. Provide the objects pictured at the bottom of the sheet. Taking each object in turn, they decide whether it is longer or shorter than their rod. They cut out the corresponding picture and glue it into the appropriate set.

Name _____ Date _____

Sorting coins

- **Sort objects**

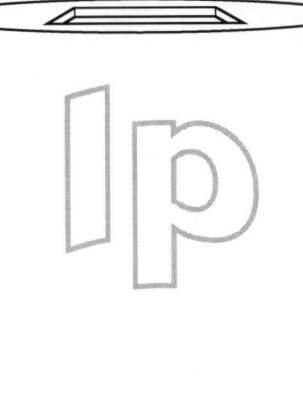  

There are ☐ 1p coins.

There are ☐ 2p coins.

There are ☐ 5p coins.

Coin	Number
1p	
2p	
5p	

You need:
- scissors
- glue

© HarperCollinsPublishers Ltd 2008

Teacher's notes
Cut out the coins and sort them into the correct money boxes.
Complete the sentences and the table.

Name _____ Date _____

Circus sorting

● **Sort objects**

JOE TOM MOL SAM MOL SAM TOM MOL TOM JOE MOL
SAM SAM TOM MOL MOL JOE SAM TOM SAM JOE

You need:

● counters ● pencil

● coloured pencils

JOE
JOE
JOE
JOE

JOE

MOL

TOM

SAM

Joe has ☐ balls.

☐ has 6 balls.

Tom has ☐ more ball than Joe.

Sam has ☐ more balls than Joe.

Teacher's notes
Choose a colour for each clown and colour their clothes and balls at the top in the same colour. Put counters on the balls, one colour at a time. Then balance the counters on the plate held by the clown. Draw round the counters and complete the sentences. Joe's have been done for you.

Name _____ Date _____

How many spans?

● Estimate, measure and compare objects

Object	My estimate	My check
string of beads	☐ hand spans	☐ hand spans
	☐ hand spans	☐ hand spans
	☐ hand spans	☐ hand spans
	☐ hand spans	☐ hand spans

Teacher's notes
Provide children with a selection of objects to be measured. They look at each object in turn and estimate the length (or length of one of its sides) as a number of hand spans and record their estimate. They then check by measuring and recording the actual number of hand spans.

Name _____ Date _____

Units of measure

● **Measure objects, choosing and using suitable measuring instruments**

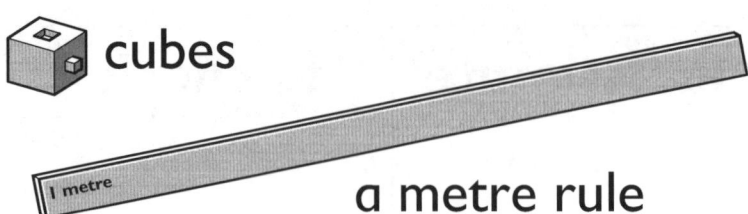 cubes

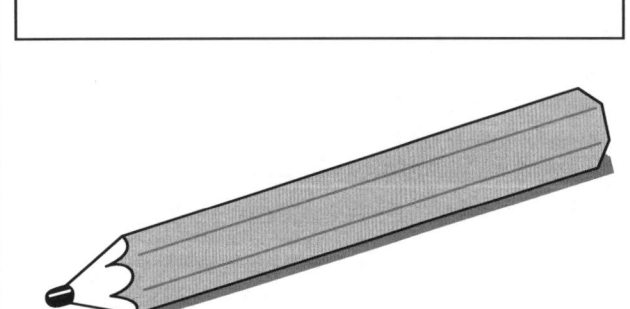 a metre rule

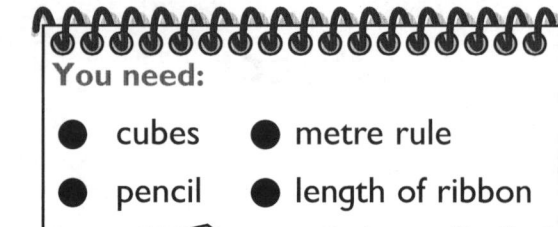
You need:
- ● cubes
- ● metre rule
- ● pencil
- ● length of ribbon

I measured a pencil, using

[ ]

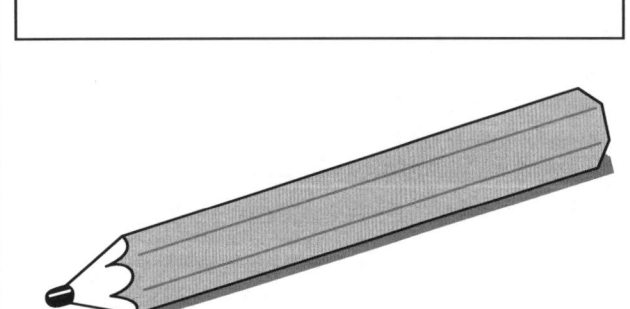

It measured [ ]

I measured the classroom, using [ ]

It measured [ ]

I measured my friend, using

[ ]

My friend measured

[ ]

I measured a ribbon, using [ ]

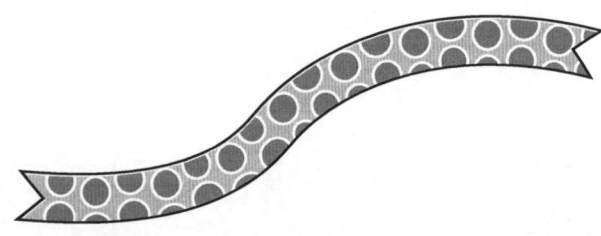

It measured [ ]

Teacher's notes
Children look at each object in turn. They decide which instrument of measure is the most appropriate for each and measure each one using their chosen instrument. They record their choice and results.

Name _____ Date _____

Sorting Smileys

● **Sort objects in different ways**

Smiley	Number		Smiley	Number

Teacher's notes
Sort the Smileys in two different ways. Draw a circle for each Smiley. Make a table for each way.

Name _____ Date _____

Word lengths

● Draw a block graph

Hickory dickory dock,
The mouse ran up the clock.
The clock struck one,
the mouse ran down.
Hickory dickory dock.

Number of words

| | 2 | 3 | 4 | 5 | 6 | 7 |

Number of letters

☐ words have 3 letters.

☐ words have 5 letters.

3 words have ☐ letters.

The most common word length is ☐ letters.

☐ words have more than 5 letters.

Teacher's notes
Count the letters in each word of the nursery rhyme. For each word, colour a block.
Cross off the word. Count the number of blocks in each column. Complete the sentences.

Name _____ Date _____

Before and after

● Order events

Before

Before

Before

After

After

After

Teacher's notes
Draw a picture which shows an event before/after the one illustrated.

Name _____ Date _____

What's next?

● **Order events**

Event A

Event B

Teacher's notes
For each event, write a number in the corner of each box to put the pictures in the right order.

Name _____   Date _____

Dan's directions

You need:
● scissors ● glue

● Use words to describe position and direction

| right | up | right | up | up | down | left | down | right |

Teacher's notes
Cut out the arrows from the bottom of the sheet and stick them on the appropriate signposts.

Name _____ Date _____

Pattern trail

You need:
● scissors ● glue

● **Use words to describe position and direction**

Theo

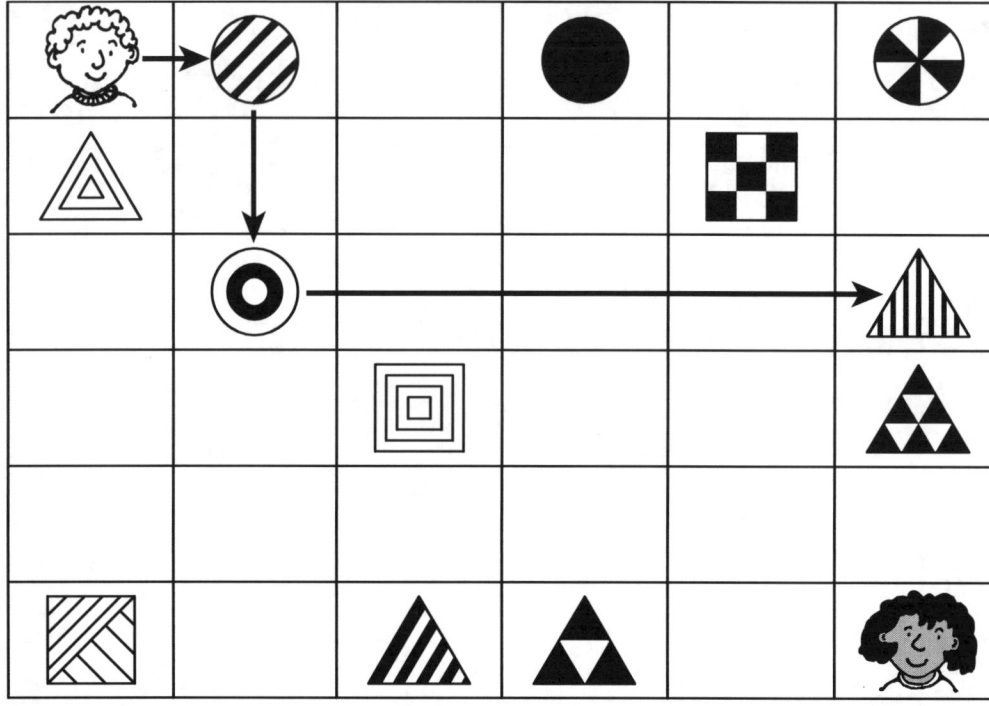

Tia

Theo's Trail

Tia's Trail

  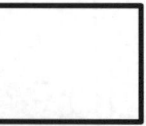    

 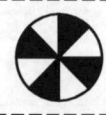 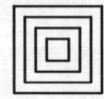   

Teacher's notes
Follow the directions given, drawing a line to find the order of Theo's and Tia's trails.
Then cut out the shapes and stick them into the spaces to show each trail.

Name _____ Date _____

Order of the day

You need:
- scissors
- glue
- large sheet of paper

● **Order events**

Teacher's notes

Look at each picture and discuss it. Cut out the pictures and place them in order.
Then stick them in that order on a large sheet of paper.
There are various possibilities for correct answers.

Name _____   Date _____

Estimating elephants

● Estimate a number of objects

Guess

◯

Now
check

☐

Guess

◯

Now
check

☐

Guess

◯

Now
check

☐

Guess

◯

Now
check

☐

Guess

◯

Now
check

☐

Guess

◯

Now
check

☐

Teacher's notes

Look quickly at the first set of elephants, then cover them and guess how many there
are. Write the guess in the circle. Now check it by counting the elephants and writing
the number in the box. Repeat for the other five sets.

Name _____ Date _____

Measuring marrows

You need:
● ruler

● **Estimate and measure objects**

Garden competition

ESTIMATES

LENGTH

◯ cm — □ cm

◯ cm — □ cm

◯ cm — □ cm

◯ cm — □ cm

◯ cm — □ cm

© HarperCollinsPublishers Ltd 2008

Teacher's notes

Look at each marrow in turn, estimating its length in centimetres. Write the estimate in the space provided then measure the length using a ruler. Record the length of each marrow in the spaces provided.

Name _____ Date _____

Rolling bowling balls

You need:
- scissors ● glue

● **Recognise and make whole and half turns**

44

Teacher's notes
Bottom section: Cut out the bowling balls.
Top section: Look at each sequence of balls. Identify the missing balls in each sequence and stick into position those that show a half turn and then a whole turn as the ball rolls towards the skittles.

Name _____ Date _____

Count the flowers in 5s

You need:
● coloured pencil

● Begin to count in fives

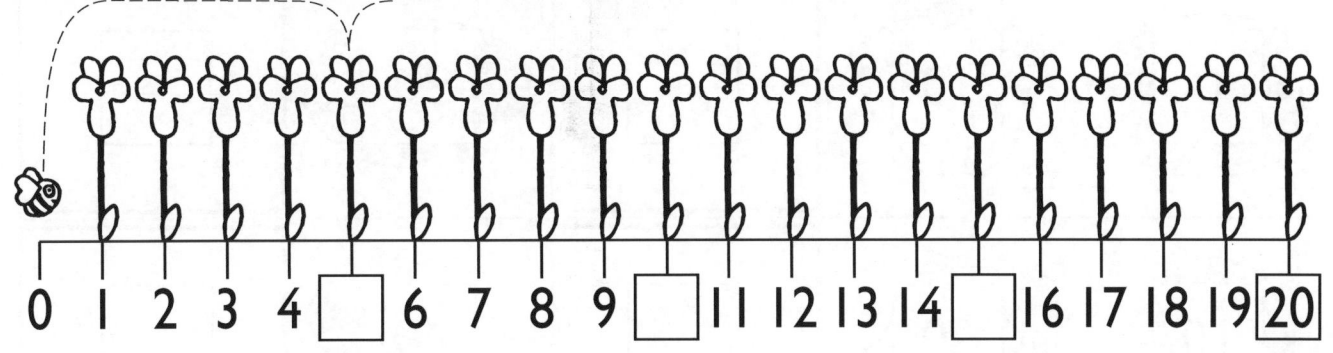

0 1 2 3 4 ☐ 6 7 8 9 ☐ 11 12 13 14 ☐ 16 17 18 19 20

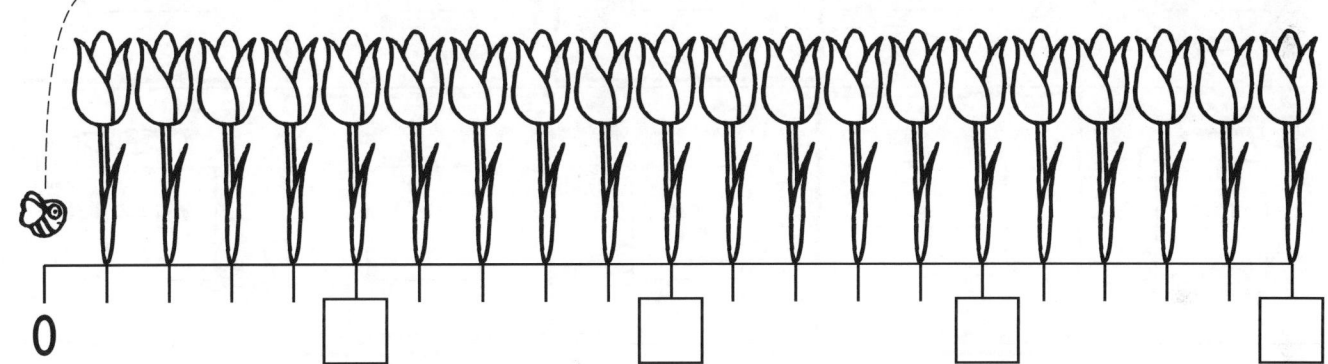

0　　　　☐　　　　☐　　　　☐　　　　☐

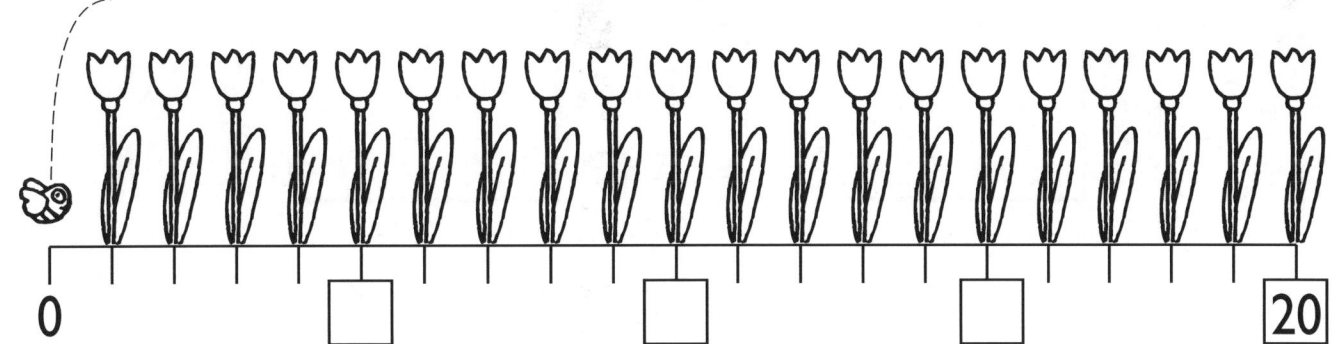

0　　　☐　　　☐　　　☐　　　20

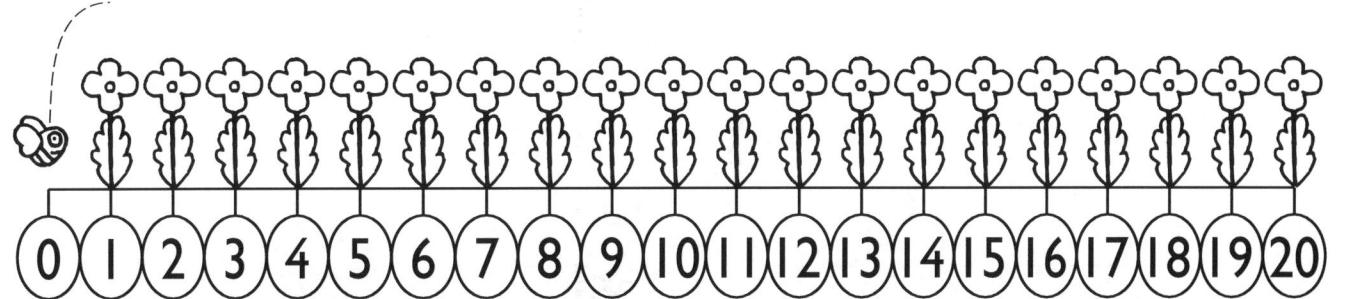

0 1 2 3 4 5 6 7 8 9 10 11 12 13 14 15 16 17 18 19 20

Teacher's notes
On each flower number line, start from zero and count on in steps of five, labelling positions 5, 10, 15 and 20. On the last number line, count in fives from zero and colour the flowers and numbers landed on.

Name _____ Date _____

Tea party tens

You need:
- scissors ● glue

● **Count on in tens**

| 0 | 10 | ☐ | 30 | ☐ |

| 10 | 20 | ☐ | 40 | ☐ |

| 50 | ☐ | 70 | ☐ | 90 |

| 60 | ☐ | 80 | ☐ | 100 |

| 30 | 60 | 20 | 50 |
| 40 | 90 | 80 | 70 |

Teacher's notes
Cut out the multiples of ten from the bottom of the sheet. Look carefully at each sequence of counting in tens, and glue each multiple into the correct position in the sequence.

46

Name _____ Date _____

Add or subtract?

● **Solve simple word problems**

Caie has 3 robots.

Leo has 2 robots.

How many robots altogether?

 + [ ] = [ ]

Rob has 7 chocolates.

He eats 4. How many are left?

[ ] − [ ] = [ ]

There were 9 cats on the wall.

3 jumped off.

How many cats were left?

 − [ ] = [ ]

How much money is in Cavan's wallet?

 + 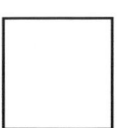 =

Teacher's notes
Look at each problem in turn, and complete the correct calculation for each problem in the spaces underneath.

Name _____ Date _____

How many socks on the line?

● **Understand addition and subtraction**

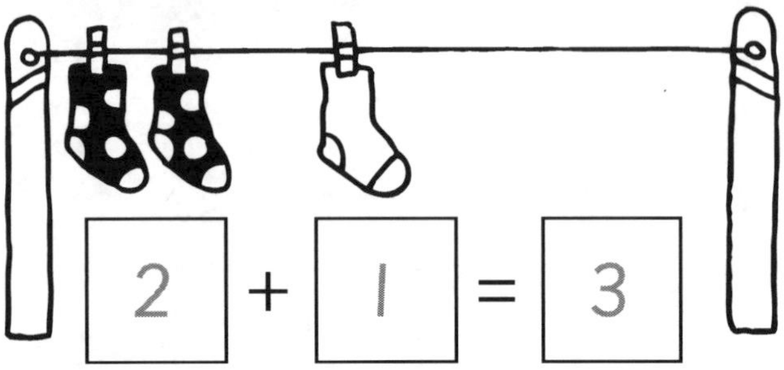

2 + 1 = 3

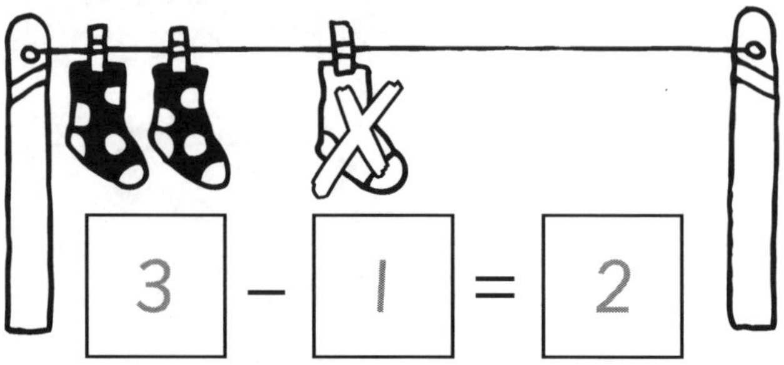

3 – 1 = 2

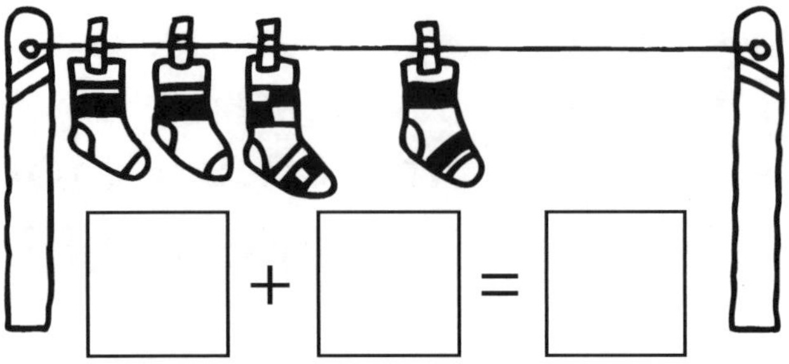

☐ + ☐ = ☐

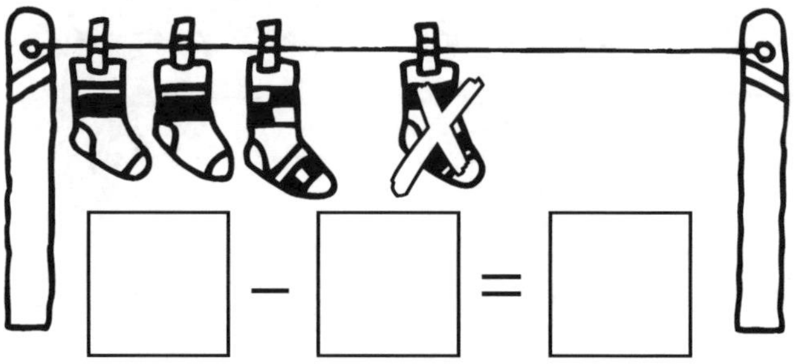

☐ – ☐ = ☐

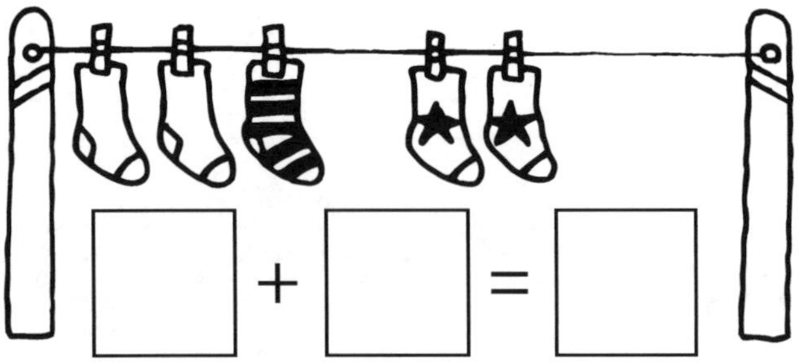

☐ + ☐ = ☐

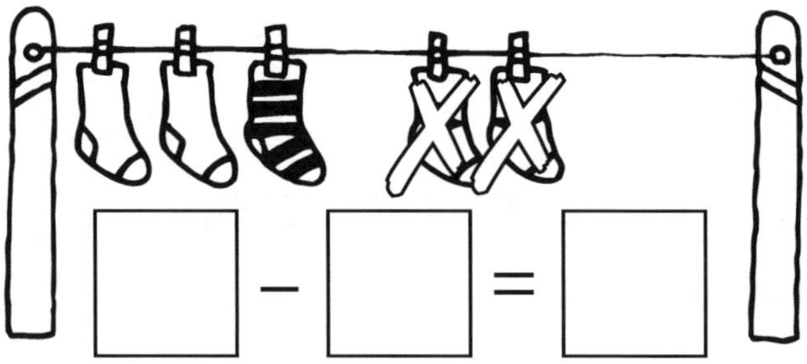

☐ – ☐ = ☐

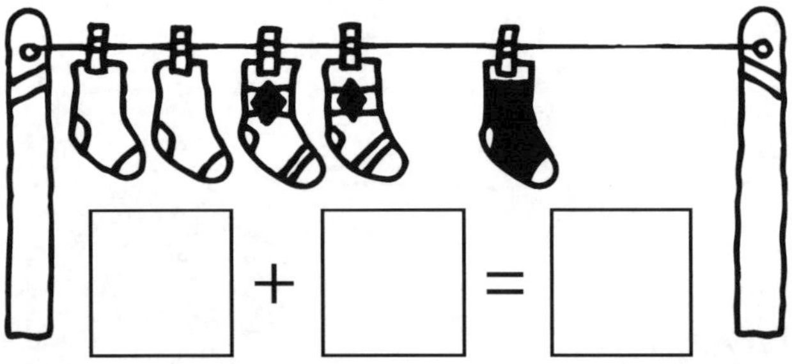

☐ + ☐ = ☐

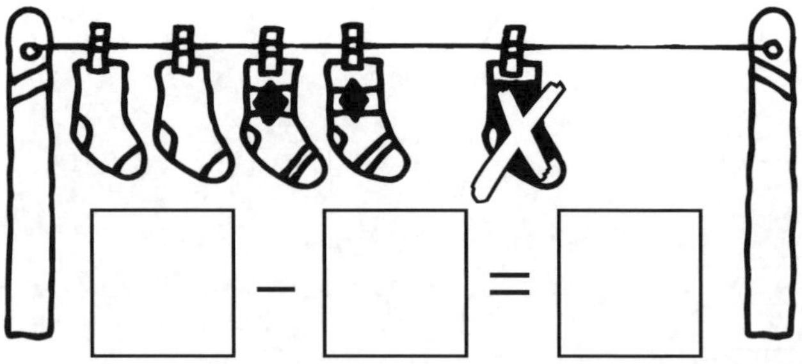

☐ – ☐ = ☐

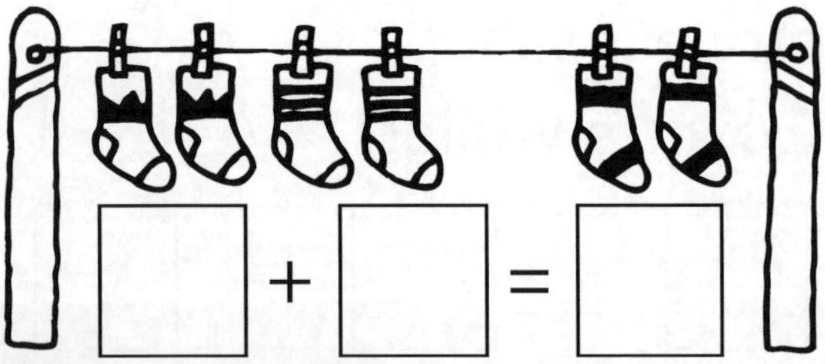

☐ + ☐ = ☐

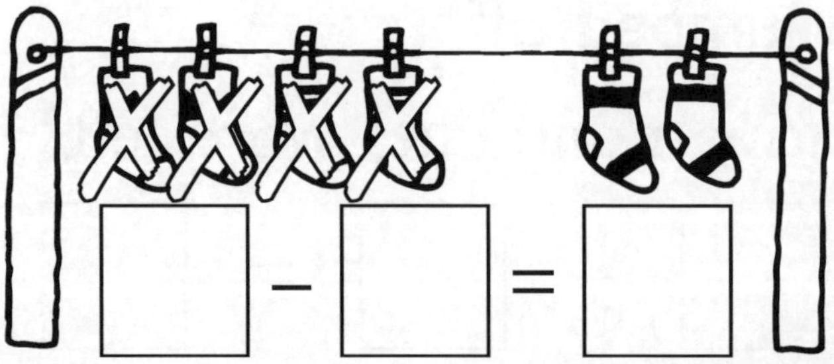

☐ – ☐ = ☐

Teacher's notes
Left section: For each line of socks, write the addition calculation.
Right section: For each line of socks, write the subtraction calculation. Then use it to check the corresponding addition.

Name _____ Date _____

Twins' birthday totals

- **Know doubles of numbers to 5 + 5**

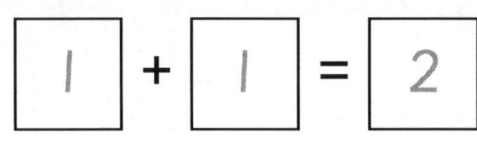

$\boxed{1} + \boxed{1} = \boxed{2}$

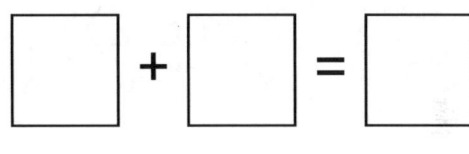

$\boxed{} + \boxed{} = \boxed{}$

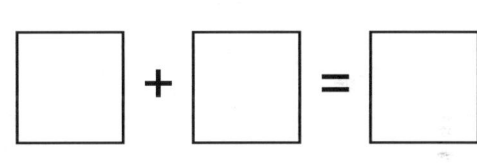

$\boxed{} + \boxed{} = \boxed{}$

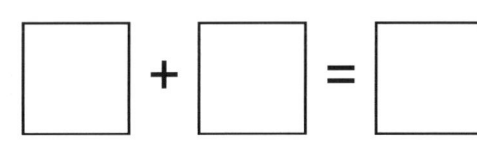

$\boxed{} + \boxed{} = \boxed{}$

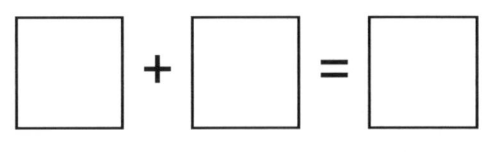

$\boxed{} + \boxed{} = \boxed{}$

Teacher's notes
For each panel, count the candles on each twin's cake and find the total number of candles. Write these three numbers in the squares to show the addition double.

Name _____ Date _____

Apple addition and subtraction

● **Add and take away numbers**

1	add 2	3
3	add 2	☐
2	add 2	☐

2	take away 1	1
5	take away 1	☐
1	take away 1	☐

2	+ 1	☐
1	+ 1	☐
4	+ 1	☐

4	− 2	☐
5	− 2	☐
3	− 2	☐

Teacher's notes
Add/subtract the number on each arrow to/from the number in the left-hand tree.
Write each answer in the corresponding right-hand tree.

Name _____ Date _____

Bracelet 5s and necklace 2s

You need:
● coloured pencil

● **Count on or back in twos or fives**

0   5   15   20   10   30   25

0   18   22   24   20   2   16   14   26   4   28   12   30   6   8   10

Teacher's notes
Draw the string to join the beads in the correct order, counting in either steps of five or steps of two. Colour the numbers that appear in both bead strings.

© HarperCollinsPublishers Ltd 2008

Name _____ Date _____

What's my number pattern?

- Count on or back in twos, fives and tens

| 0 | 5 | 10 | | | | | | | 50 |

| 0 | 2 | | | | | | | | | 20 |

| 0 | 10 | | | | 50 |

| 20 | 18 | | | | | | | | 0 |

| 50 | 40 | | | | |

| 50 | 45 | | | | | | 0 |

Teacher's notes
Identify the number pattern on each scarf, counting on or back in 2s, 5s or 10s.
Write the correct numbers in the spaces provided.

Name _____ Date _____

Cake cutting

● **Find half of a shape**

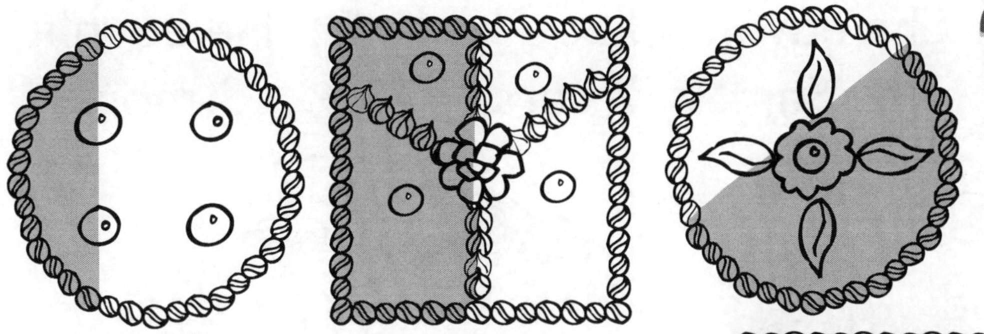

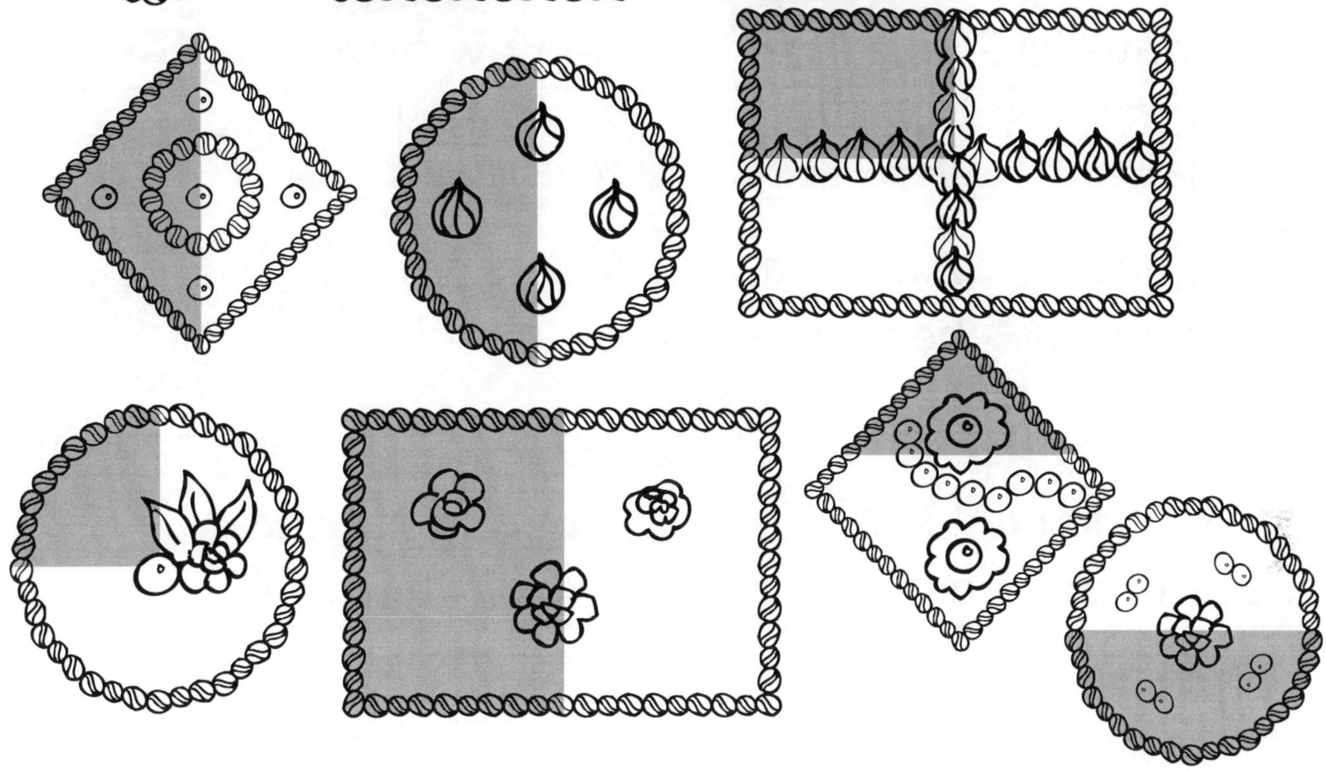

© HarperCollinsPublishers Ltd 2008

Teacher's notes
Top section: Colour the cakes that have been cut in half.
Bottom section: Draw a line to cut each cake in half. Colour one half of each cake.

Name _____ Date _____

Some word problems

- **Solve simple word problems**

Samira had 9 sweets. She gave 3 to Sam.

How many did she have left?

9	$\ominus$	3	=	6

Leon had 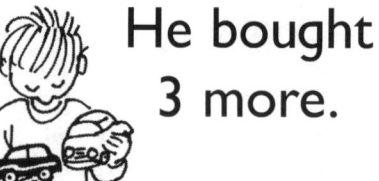 He bought 3 more.
7 cars.

How many cars does he now have?

	$\bigcirc$		=	

Lucy had 4 flowers. Amina gave her 5 more.

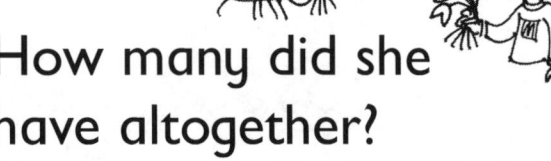

How many did she have altogether?

	$\bigcirc$		=	

9 cats sat on a wall.

2 jumped off.

How many were left on the wall?

	$\bigcirc$		=	

Imran had 10 buttons on his shirt. 2 fell off.

How many buttons were left?

	$\bigcirc$		=	

Carla had 5 marbles.  Tim had 5 marbles.

How many marbles altogether?

	$\bigcirc$		=	

Teacher's notes
Read each problem, using the illustrations where necessary. Then write out the
calculation in the boxes below.

Name _____ Date _____

Sandcastle calculations

You need:
● scissors ● glue

● **Add two numbers**

1 + 1 = ☐

3 + 2 = ☐

2 + ☐ = 3

4 + 0 = ☐

5 + 1 = ☐

4 + ☐ = 7

2 + ☐ = 9

6 + 2 = ☐

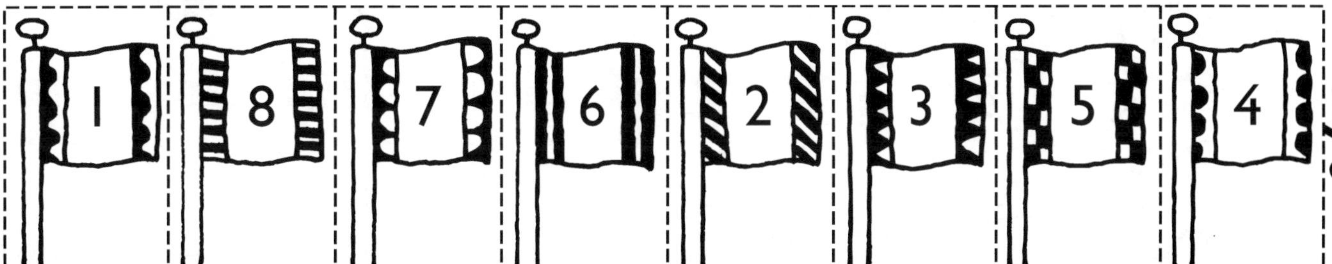

Flags: 1   8   7   6   2   3   5   4

Teacher's notes
Cut out the pictures of the answer flags from the bottom of the sheet. Then, for each addition calculation, stick the correct flag in the space provided.

Name _____ Date _____

Snail trail subtraction

● **Subtract two numbers**

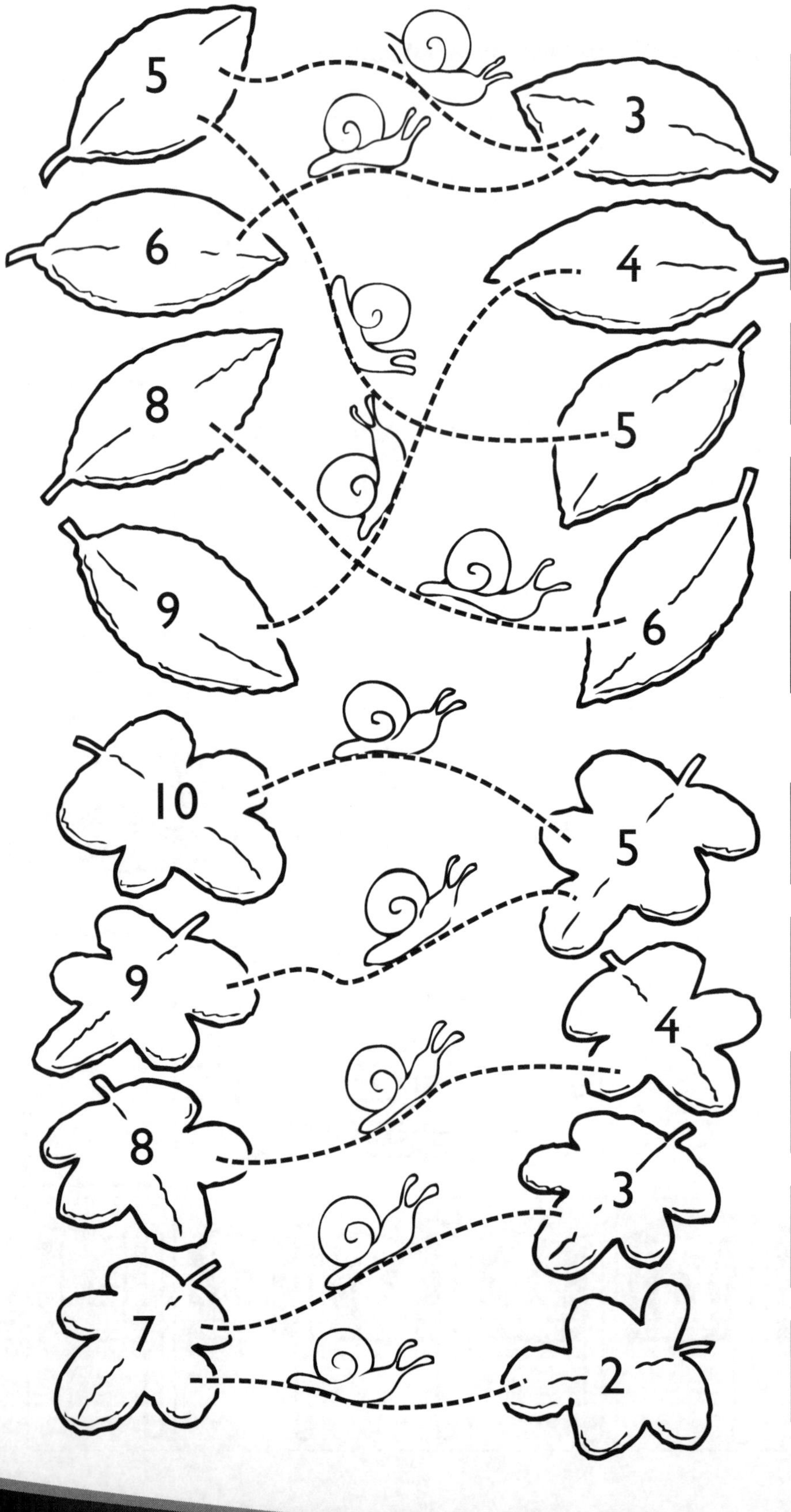

| 5 | − | 3 | = | |

| | − | | = | |

| | − | | = | |

| | − | | = | |

| | − | | = | |

| 10 | − | 5 | = | |

| | − | | = | |

| | − | | = | |

| | − | | = | |

| | − | | = | |

© HarperCollinsPublishers Ltd 2008

Teacher's notes
Trace over each snail trail, for example, from 10 to 5, and write the subtraction calculation
and answer in the spaces provided.

Name _____ Date _____

Crab tens and sea slug units

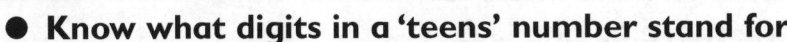
You need:
● scissors ● glue

● **Know what digits in a 'teens' number stand for**

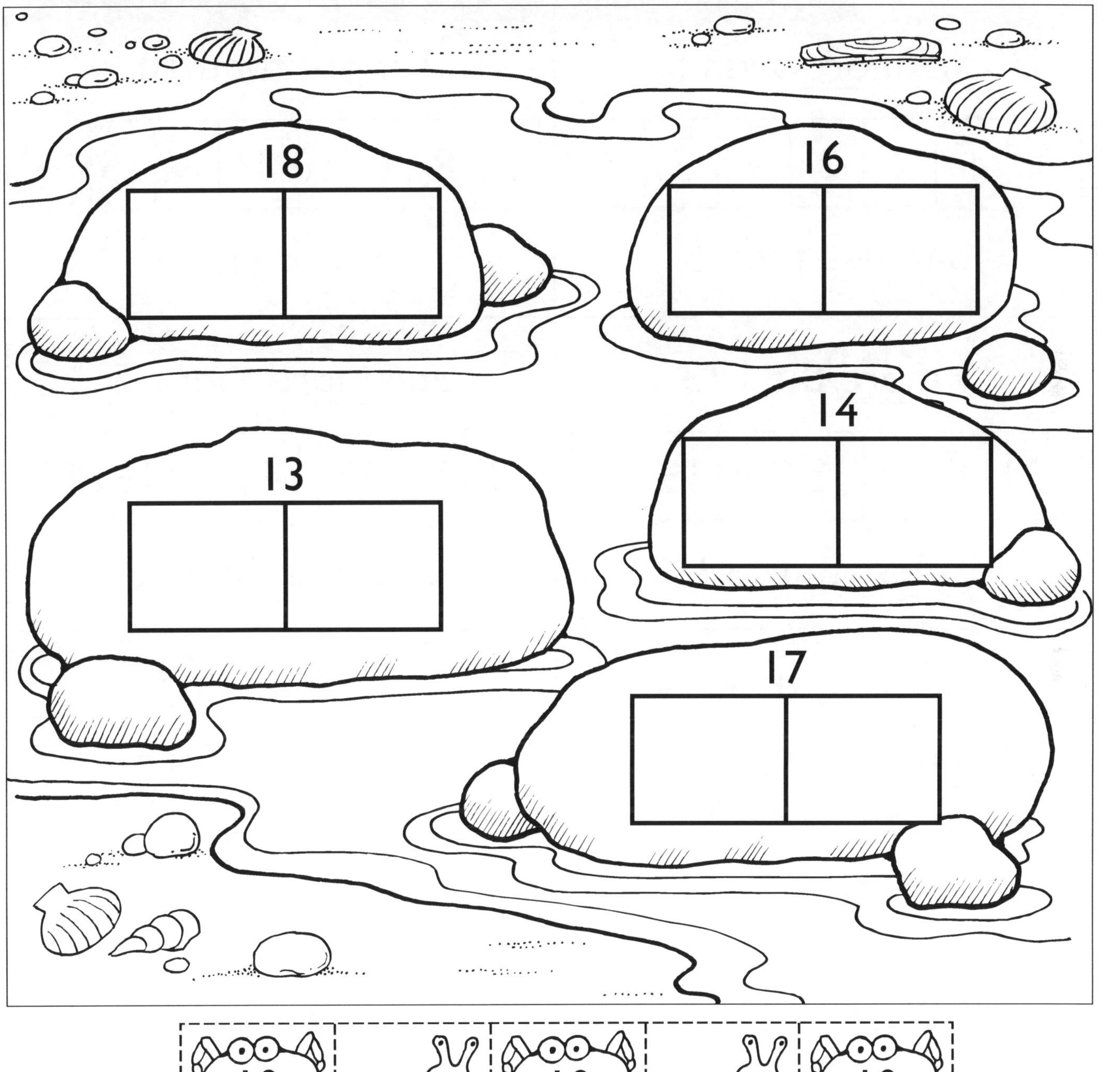

18

16

13

14

17

10 8 10 6 10

10 3 4 7 10

Teacher's notes
Cut out the tens (crabs) and units (sea slugs) from the bottom of this sheet. Stick these
onto the rocks in the rock pool according to the teens number on each rock.

© HarperCollinsPublishers Ltd 2008

Name _____ Date _____

Count on and colour

You need:
- red, green and yellow pencil

- **Know the number that is one more or one less**

one more than 5	1 more than 10
0 1 2 3 4 5 6	7 8 9 10 11 12 13 14
one less than 5	1 less than 10
1 more than 13	one more than 15
10 11 12 13 14 15 16	11 12 13 14 15 16 17
1 less than 13	one less than 15
one more than 19	1 more than 21
14 15 16 17 18 19 20	17 18 19 20 21 22 23
one less than 19	1 less than 21
1 more than 25	1 more than 29
22 23 24 25 26 27 28	24 25 28 27 28 29 30
1 less than 25	1 less than 29

Teacher's notes
Find the number specified for each segment of the number track and circle it in red.
Then colour the number that is one less in green and the number that is one more in yellow.

Name _____ Date _____

Take away magic

● Know subtraction facts to 10

What's left over?

Example

5 – 2 = [3]

5 – 4 = [ ]

6 – 2 = [ ]

6 – 1 = [ ]

7 – 3 = [ ]

7 – 0 = [ ]

8 – 3 = [ ]

8 – 1 = [ ]

9 – 3 = [ ]

9 – 2 = [ ]

10 – 3 = [ ]

© HarperCollinsPublishers Ltd 2008

Teacher's notes
Find the missing number in each subtraction fact and write it in the square. Show this
by crossing out the appropriate bands on the wands.

Name _____ Date _____

How much is in my purse?

You need:
● scissors

● **Solve problems using money**

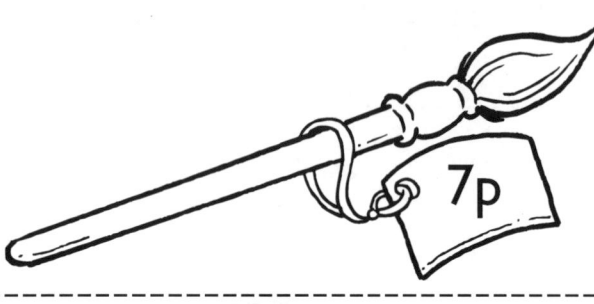

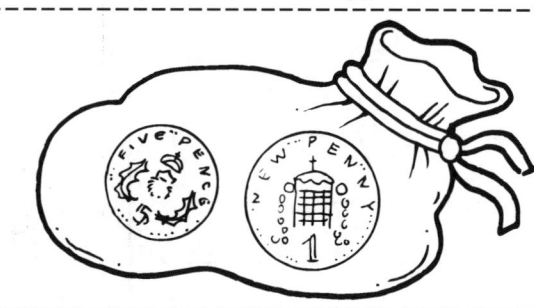

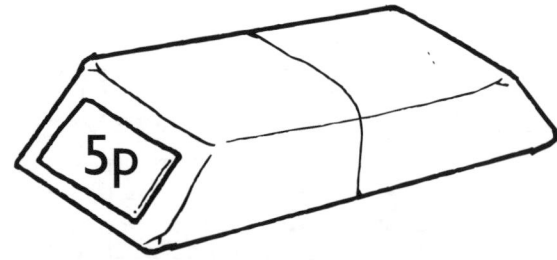
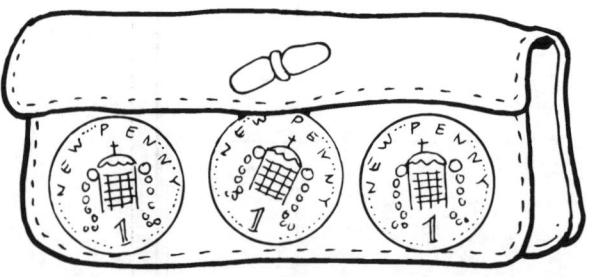

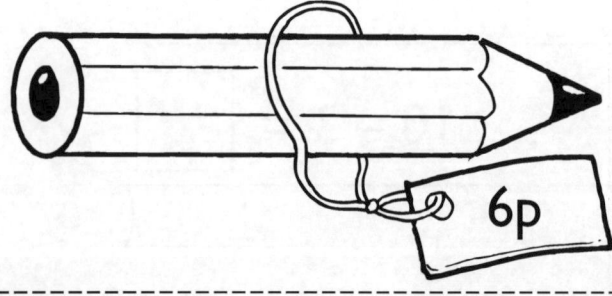

Teacher's notes
Cut out all the pictures of purses and priced items. Then match the price on each item to the value of coins in a purse.

Name _____ Date _____

Bowling scores

● **Know what each digit in a two-digit number stands for**

15

is the same as

1	and	5
ten		units

13

is the same as

	and	
ten		units

17

is the same as

	and	
ten		units

20

is the same as

	and	
tens		units

21

is the same as

	and	
tens		units

24

is the same as

	and	
tens		units

You need:
● scissors ● glue

7	2	3	2	1	2	1	0	1	1	5	4

© HarperCollinsPublishers Ltd 2008

Teacher's notes
Cut out the numbers from the bottom of the sheet. For each score, stick the correct
numbers in the tens and units boxes below.

Name _____ Date _____

Sort the orders

● **Order numbers to 20**

© HarperCollinsPublishers Ltd 2008

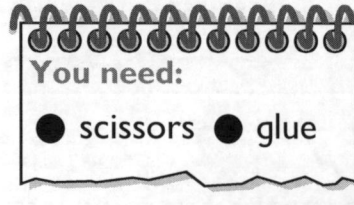

You need:
● scissors ● glue

Teacher's notes
Look at each set of three numbers. Cut the missing numbers from the bottom of the sheet to order the numbers smallest to largest.

Name _____ Date _____

Which one is easier?

You need:
● coloured pencil

● **Add two numbers**

$4 + 2 =$ ☐

$2 + 4 =$ ☐

$6 + 2 =$ ☐

$2 + 6 =$ ☐

$3 + 7 =$ ☐

$7 + 3 =$ ☐

$1 + 5 =$ ☐

$5 + 1 =$ ☐

$1 + 9 =$ ☐

$9 + 1 =$ ☐

$7 + 2 =$ ☐

$2 + 7 =$ ☐

$5 + 3 =$ ☐

$3 + 5 =$ ☐

© HarperCollinsPublishers Ltd 2008

Teacher's notes
Complete the addition calculations, writing the answers in the boxes. For each pair of
number sentences, colour the answer box of the number sentence that was easier to do.

Name _____ Date _____

Make money!

● **Solve problems using money**

Make 5p

Use 3 coins

Make 7p

Use 2 coins

Make 6p

Use 3 coins

Make 10p

Use 5 coins

Make 8p

Use the fewest coins

© HarperCollinsPublishers Ltd 2008

Teacher's notes
Draw and label the given number of coins whose values add up to the sum of money.
The coins can be represented by labelled plain circles.

Name _____ Date _____

Team of trios

You need:
● scissors ● glue

● **Know the names of 2-D shapes**

More than 3 sides team

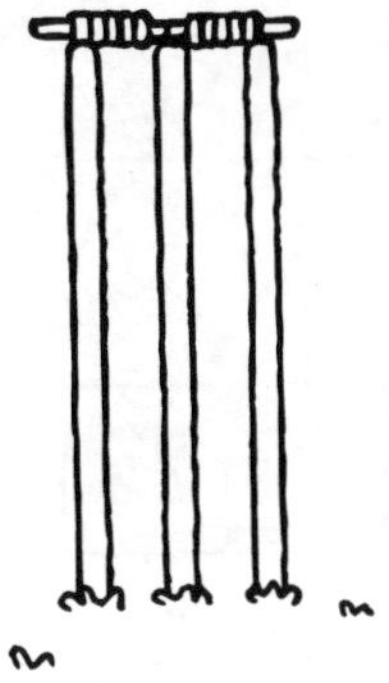

Less than 3 sides team

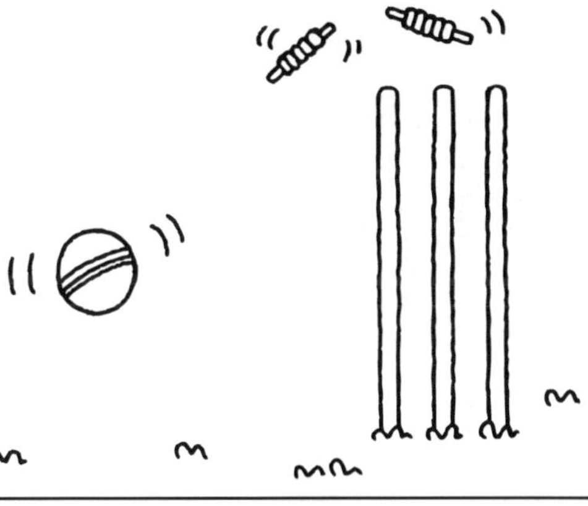

Exactly 3 sides team

SCOREBOARD

Teacher's notes
Cut out the players from the bottom of this sheet and put them into the correct team,
according to the shape shown on each of their shirts.

Name _____ Date _____

Count on or back and colour

You need:
● coloured pencil

● **Say the number that is 1 or 10 more or less**

1 more than 2   10 more than 0

0	1	2	3	4	5	6	7	8	9	10	11	12

1 more than 14   10 more than 10

8	9	10	11	12	13	14	15	16	17	18	19	20	21	22

1 more than 27   10 more than 20

18	19	20	21	22	23	24	25	26	27	28	29	30	31	32

1 less than 31   10 less than 30

20	21	22	23	24	25	26	27	28	29	30	31	32	33	34

1 less than 35   10 less than 40

29	30	31	32	33	34	35	36	37	38	39	40	41	42

1 less than 43   10 less than 50

37	38	39	40	41	42	43	44	45	46	47	48	49	50

Teacher's notes
Count on or back in steps of one and ten from the given starting number.
Then colour that number.

Name _____ Date _____

Bead addition

● **Add two numbers**

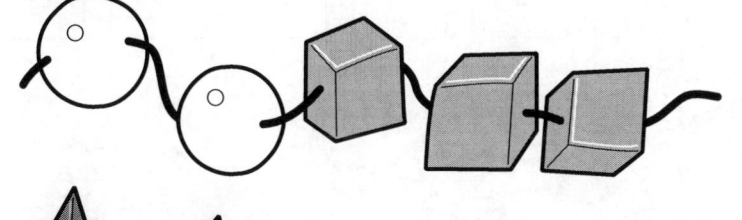

| 1 | + | 4 | = | |

| | + | | = | |

| | + | | = | |

| | + | | = | |

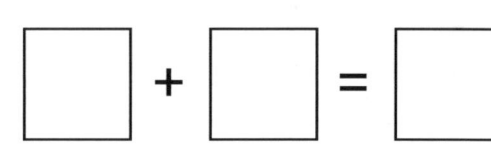

| | + | | = | |

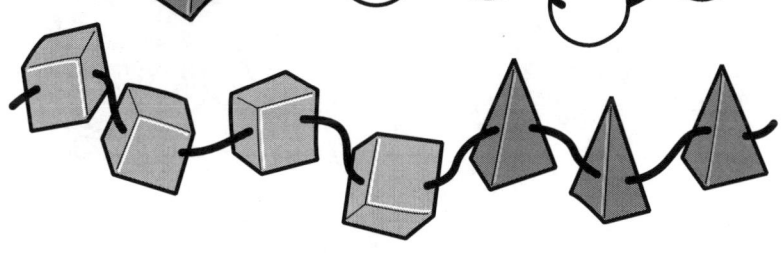

| | + | | = | |

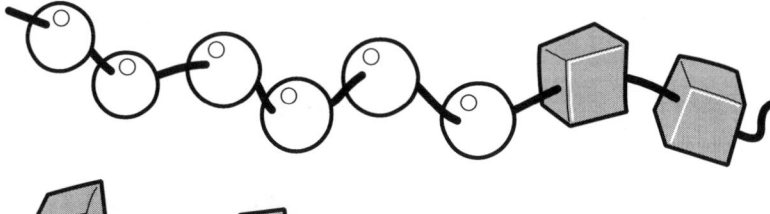

| | + | | = | |

| | + | | = | |

Teacher's notes
Look at each string of beads. Count the number of beads of each shape. Then write
the two numbers in the correct boxes and complete the addition calculation.

Name _____ Date _____

Jungle subtraction

● **Work out answers to subtraction number sentences**

0   1   2   3   4   5   6   7   8   9   10

3 − 1 = ☐

7 − 1 = ☐

4 − 3 = ☐

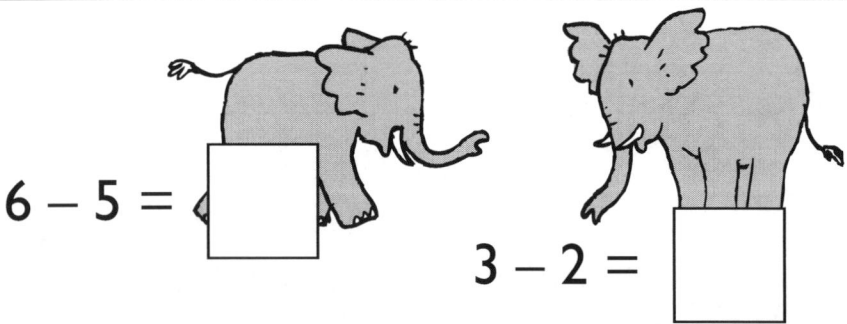
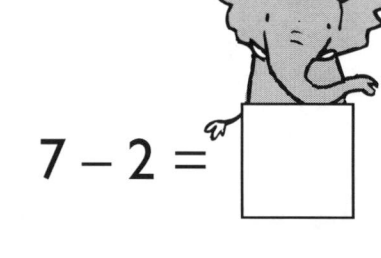

6 − 5 = ☐

3 − 2 = ☐

7 − 2 = ☐

7 − 4 = ☐

6 − 4 = ☐

5 − 2 = ☐

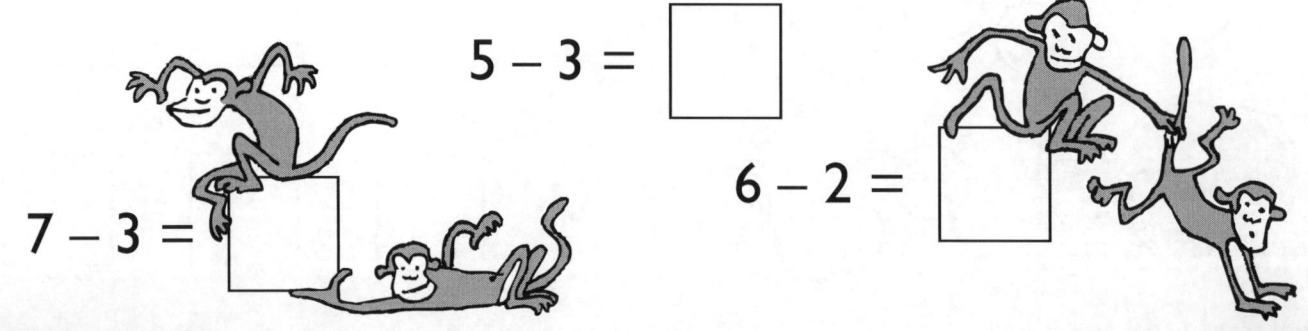

5 − 3 = ☐

6 − 2 = ☐

7 − 3 = ☐

Teacher's notes
Write the missing numbers for the subtraction number sentences in the boxes provided.

Name _____ Date _____

Make 5 and a bit with beads

● **Solve number puzzles**

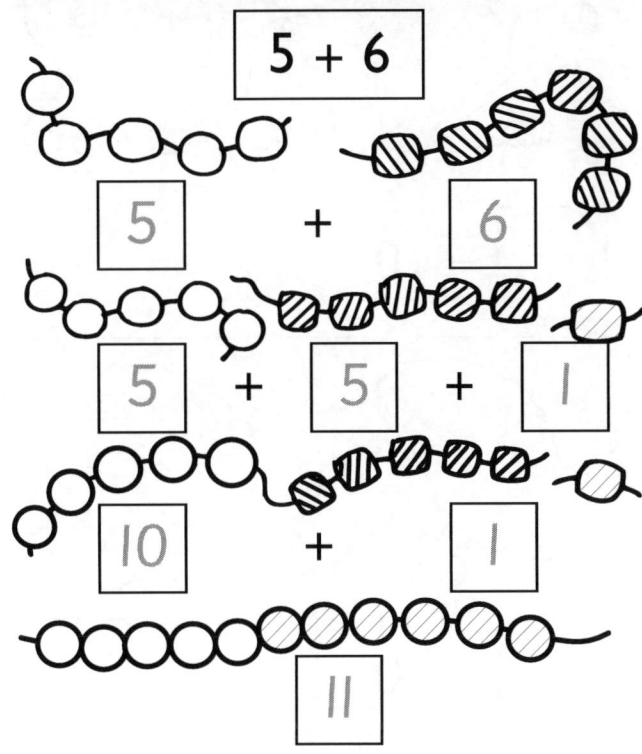

5 + 6

5 + 6

5 + 5 + 1

10 + 1

11

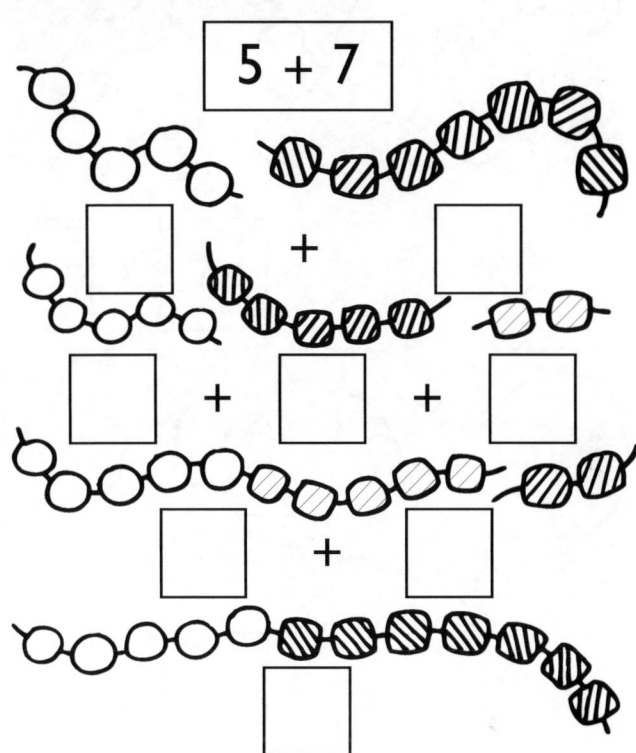

5 + 7

☐ + ☐

☐ + ☐ + ☐

☐ + ☐

☐

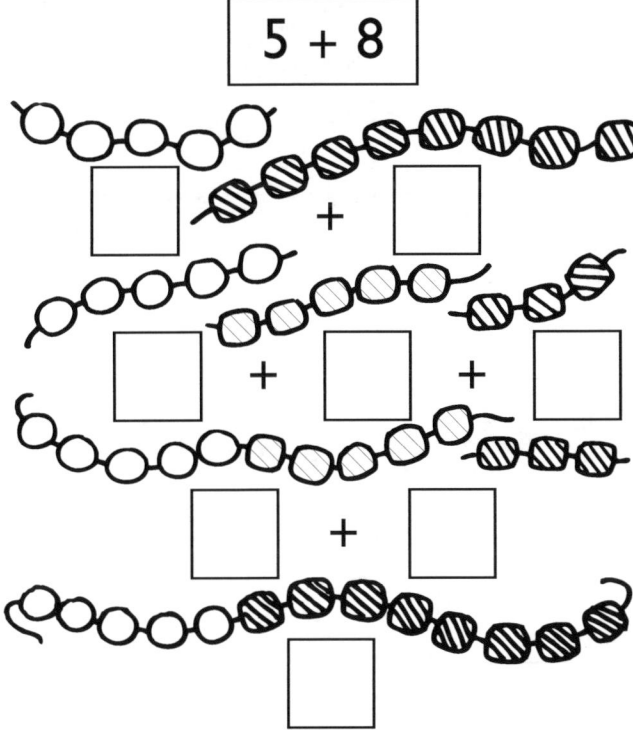

5 + 8

☐ + ☐

☐ + ☐ + ☐

☐ + ☐

☐

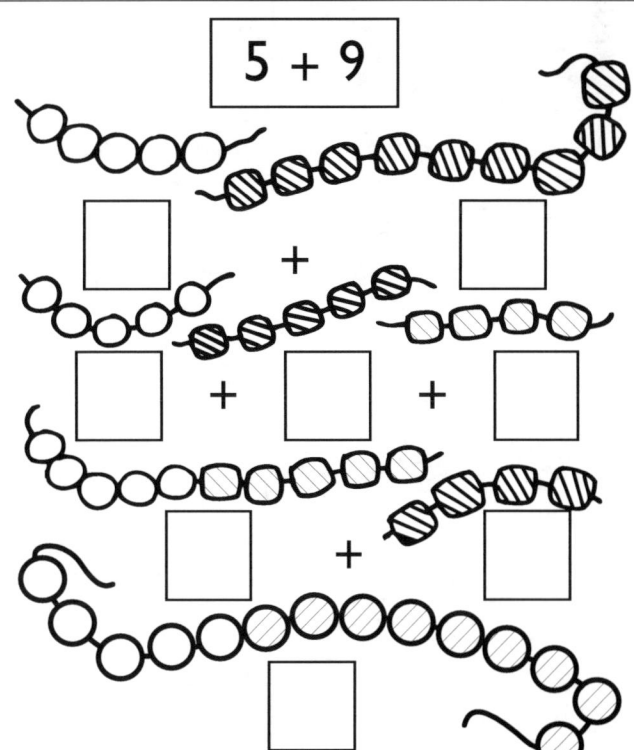

5 + 9

☐ + ☐

☐ + ☐

☐ + ☐

☐

© HarperCollinsPublishers Ltd 2008

Teacher's notes
Count the beads above the boxes. Then write in the boxes the number of beads on each string as they are threaded together.

Name _____ Date _____

Moon monsters

- Solve number puzzles

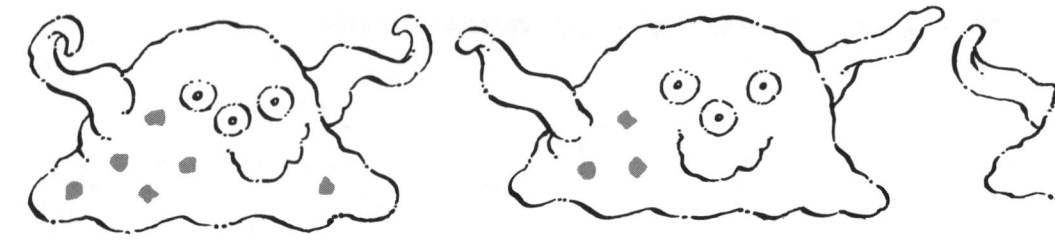

$$6 + 3 + 1 = 10$$

$$\square + \square + \square = 10$$

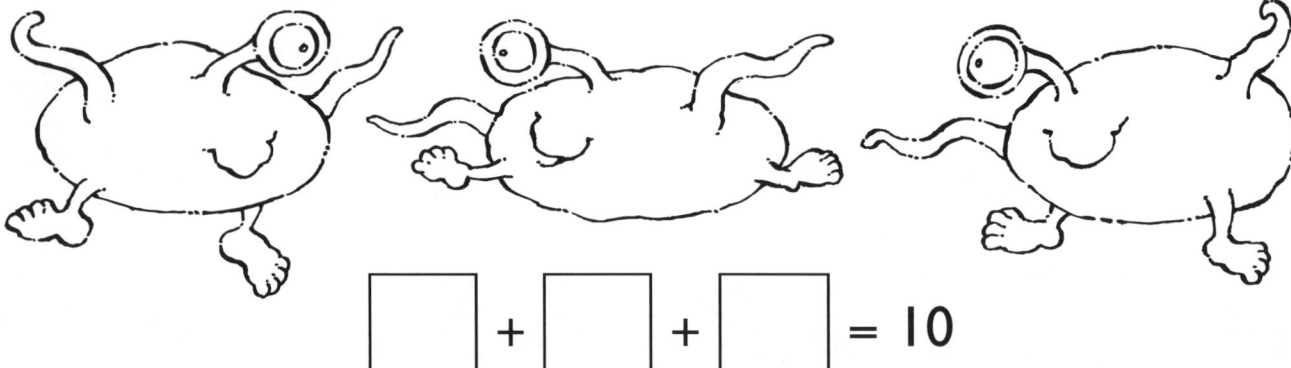

$$\square + \square + \square = 10$$

$$\square + \square + \square = 10$$

Teacher's notes
In each row, put spots on the moon monsters to make a total of 10.
Then write out the addition calculation in the boxes.

Name _____ Date _____

Pattern pathways

● Use shapes to make patterns

You need:

● scissors ● glue

Teacher's notes

Cut out the shapes from the bottom of the sheet and stick them into the spaces to complete the pattern on each pathway.

Name ____________________ Date ____________

Super shape sorters

You need:

- scissors
- glue

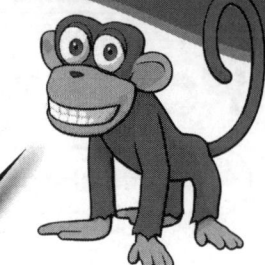

- **Know the names of common 3-D shapes**

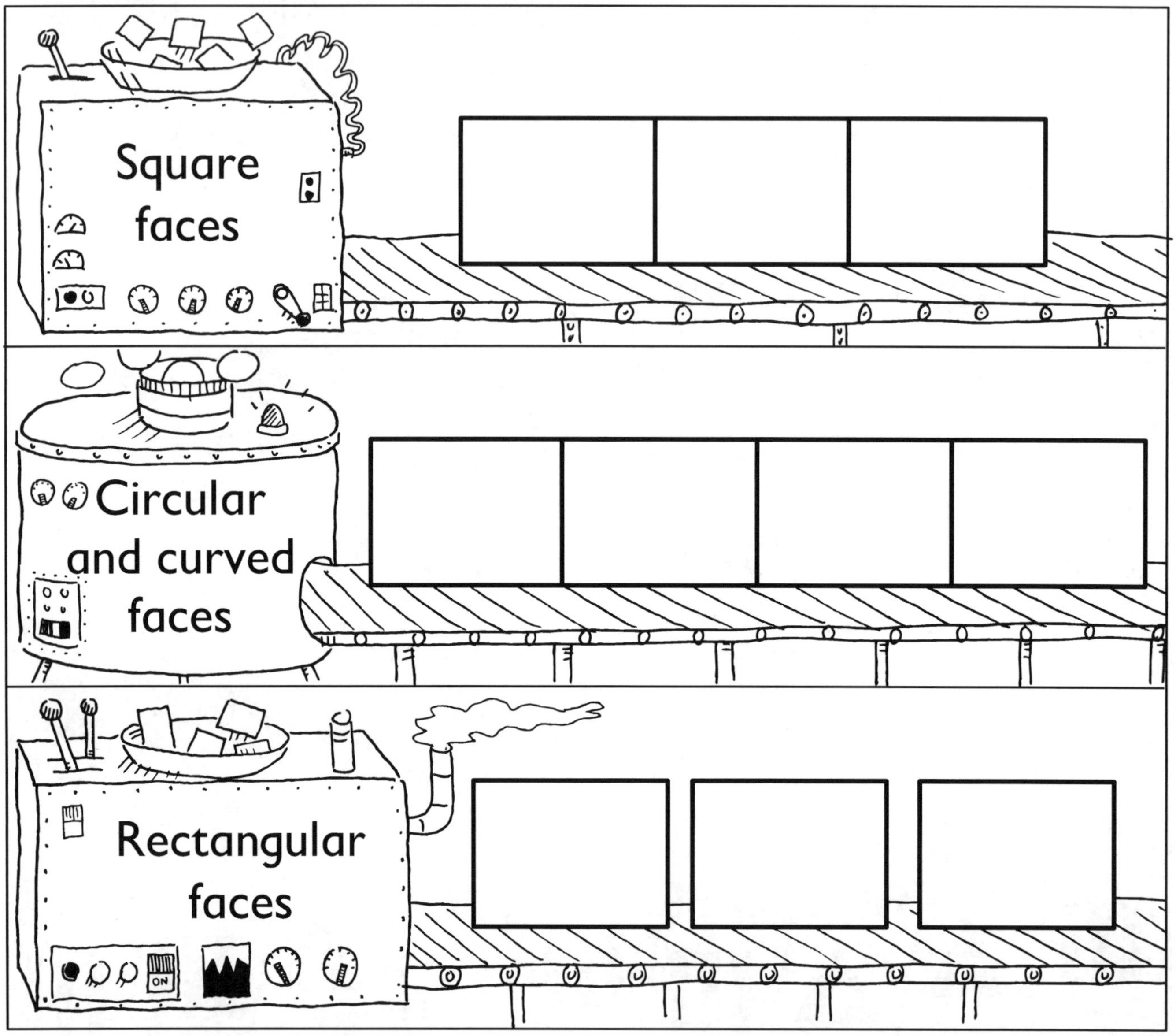
Square faces
Circular and curved faces
ON
Rectangular faces

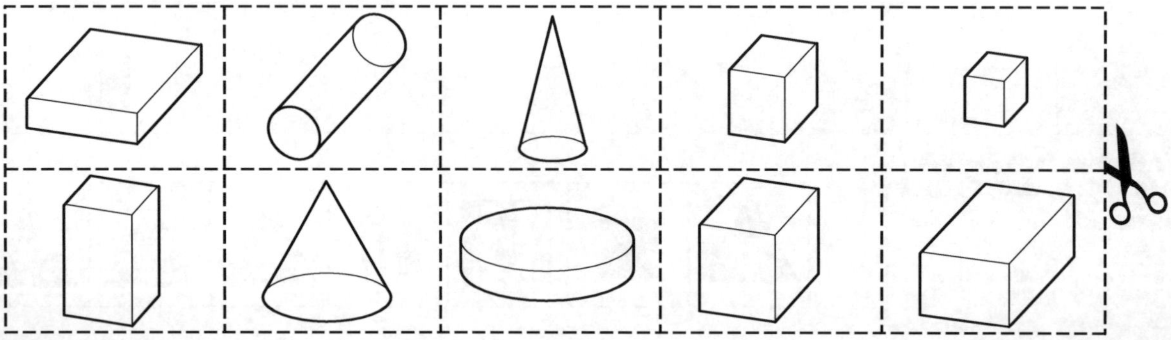

Teacher's notes

Cut out the 3-D shapes from the bottom of the sheet and stick them into the appropriate sorting machines, according to the shapes on the faces of each.

Name _____ Date _____

Matching pairs of 10

● **Know pairs of numbers that total 10**

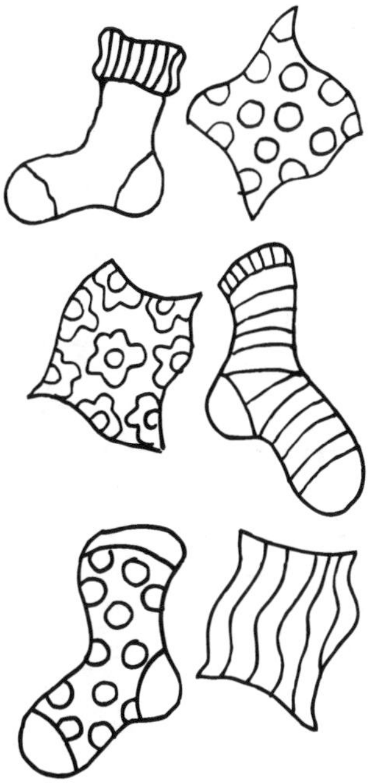

Top line numbers: 5 0 6 8 3 9 1 2

Bottom line numbers: 7 4 1 9 2 5 8 10

8	+	2	=	10
[ ]	+	[ ]	=	[ ]
[ ]	+	[ ]	=	[ ]
[ ]	+	[ ]	=	[ ]

[ ]	+	[ ]	=	[ ]
[ ]	+	[ ]	=	[ ]
[ ]	+	[ ]	=	[ ]
[ ]	+	[ ]	=	[ ]

Teacher's notes

Top section: Match the socks and handkerchiefs on the top washing line to those on the bottom washing line so that the numbers in each pair total 10.

Bottom section: Write out the corresponding addition calculation in the spaces provided.

Name _____ Date _____

Patterns of number facts

You need:
● scissors ● glue

● See patterns in number facts

7	$7 + 0 = 7$	 7	$7 - 0 = 7$

8	$8 + 0 = 8$	 8	$8 - 0 = 8$

$6 + 1 = 7$	$4 + 3 = 7$	$7 - 1 = 6$	$7 - 2 = 5$
$6 + 2 = 8$	$5 + 2 = 7$	$8 - 2 = 6$	$7 - 3 = 4$
$7 + 1 = 8$	$5 + 3 = 8$	$8 - 3 = 5$	$8 - 1 = 7$

Teacher's notes
Cut out the number facts of seven and eight from the bottom of the sheet and sort them into addition and subtraction sets for each of these numbers. Then stick each fact on the appropriate quilt in the correct order.

Name _____ Date _____

Double trouble!

You need:
● scissors ● glue

● Know doubles of numbers up to 5 + 5 or more

2 | 1 1 | 1 + 1

4

6

8

10

12

14

✂

1 + 1	7 + 7	4 + 4	6 + 6	2 + 2	5 + 5	3 + 3
2 3	1 6	5 2	1 4	3 7	6 4	7 5

Teacher's notes
The Magician's doubles spells are mixed up. Cut out the stars from the bottom of glue sheet and match each addition double to its answer on a cauldron. Then cut out the matching calculation and place this underneath. The stick each star and calculation in place.

© HarperCollinsPublishers Ltd 2008

75

Name _____ Date _____

Trees of 12

- **Solve number puzzles**

Teacher's notes
On each tree, each line (two diagonal and one horizontal) of three apples adds up to
12. Find the missing number in each line and write it on the empty apple.

Name _____ Date _____

Heavier and lighter

You need:
● red and yellow coloured pencils

● **Compare the weights of two objects**

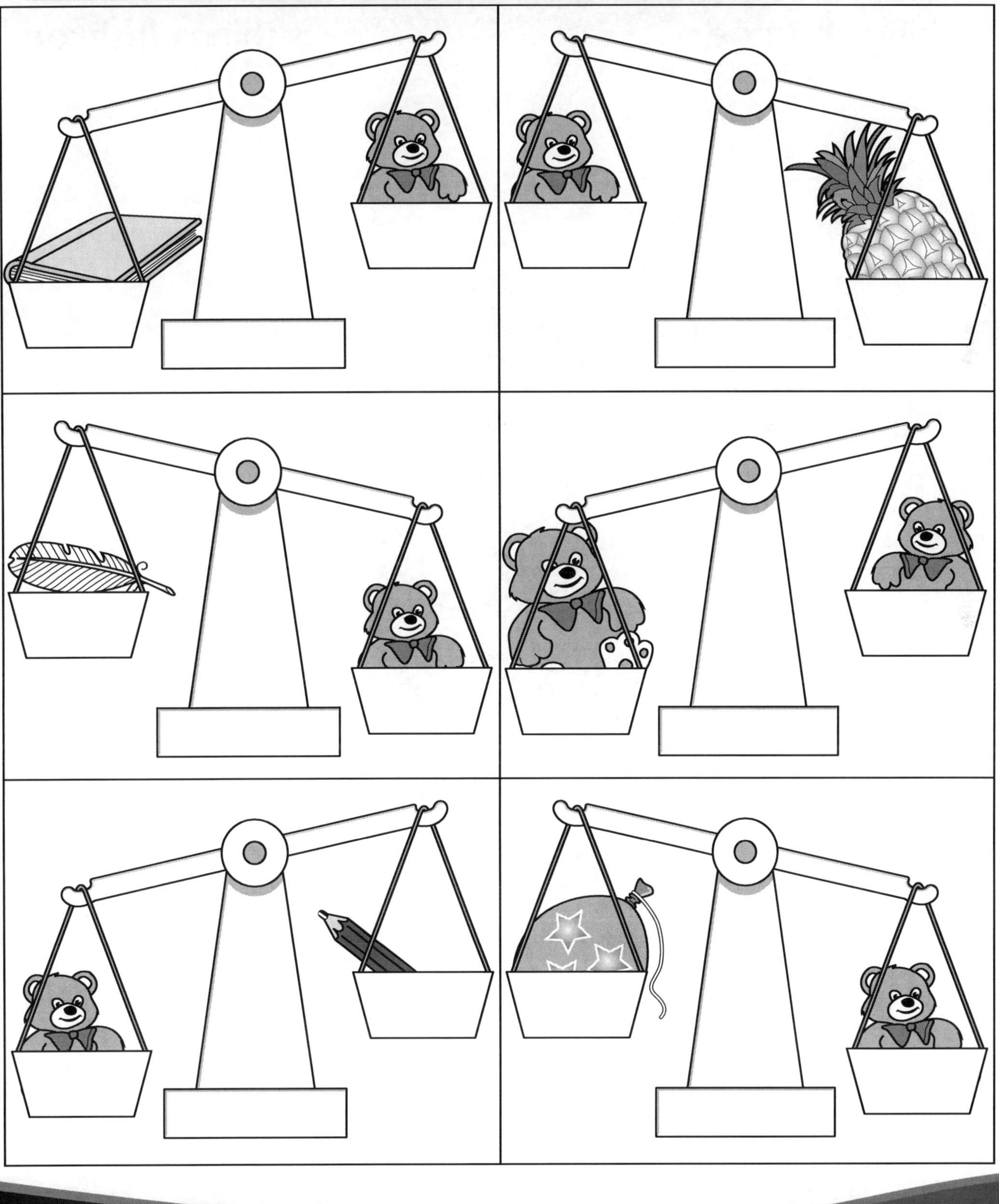

Teacher's notes
Which balance shows objects that are heavier than the teddy and which shows
objects that are lighter? Colour the pan with the heavier item in red and the pan with
the lighter item in yellow.

Name _____ Date _____

Weigh the shoe

You need:
- 6 objects
- balance
- your shoe

● **Compare weights**

3 things **heavier**

3 things **lighter**

My shoe

Teacher's notes

Choose three objects which seem to be heavier than your shoe, and three objects which seem to be lighter. Name or draw each of them in the spaces provided. Then, using a balance, check these predictions. Put a tick in the box if the prediction is correct or a cross if it is wrong.

Name _____ Date _____

Sorting creatures

You need:
● scissors ● glue

● **Sort objects by placing them on a diagram**

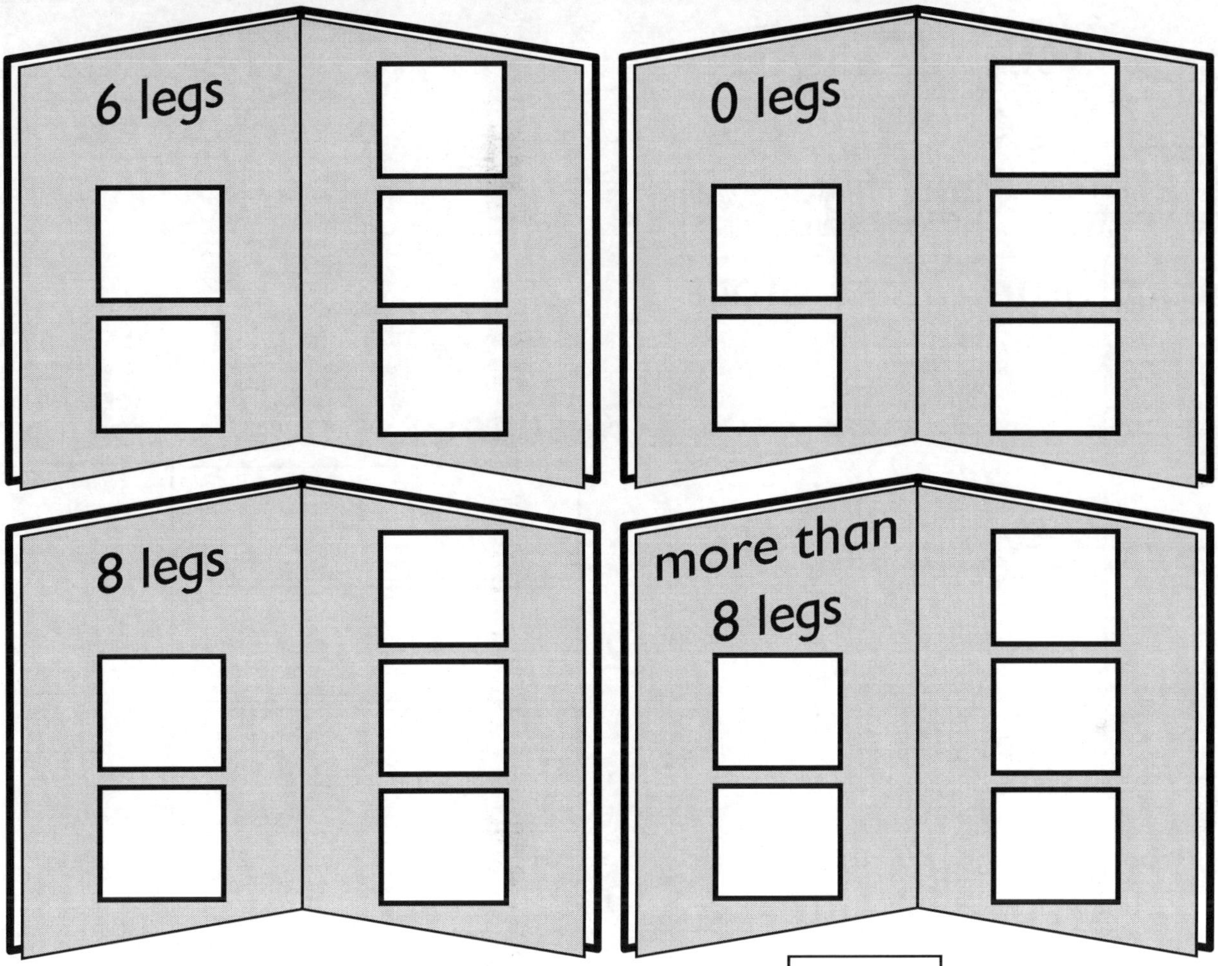

6 legs

0 legs

8 legs

more than 8 legs

How many creatures have 6 legs?

How many creatures have no legs?

How many creatures have more than 8 legs?

How many creatures have less than 8 legs?

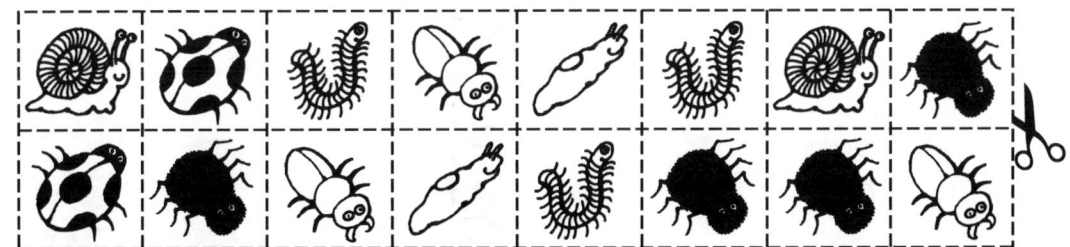

Teacher's notes
Cut out the creatures from the bottom of the sheet and sort them into sets, then stick
them in the appropriate books. Then complete the sentences.

Name _____ Date _____

Race results

You need:
- 4 counters
- 1–6 dice

- **Show what happened using lists**

Mac	Val	Hal	Tom
Start	Start	Start	Start
Finish	Finish	Finish	Finish

Results

1. _____

2. _____

3. _____

4. _____

The winner is _____ .

_____ came last.

_____ came fourth.

The third runner to finish was

_____ .

Teacher's notes
Work in groups of four. Choose a character and a counter and place the counter on 'start'.
Take it in turns to roll the dice and move the counter. Write the name of each character as
she or he finishes the race.

Name _____ Date _____

Heaviest or lightest?

You need:
- 9 objects
- balance

- **Compare the weights of more than two objects and put them in order**

SET 1

heaviest		lightest

SET 2

heaviest		lightest

SET 3

heaviest		lightest

Teacher's notes
Provide children with three sets, each with three objects of differing weights.
They compare the weight of each of the three objects in each set and record their findings.

Name _____ Date _____

Which is heavier?
Which is lighter?

● **Compare the weights of two objects**

The [   ] is balanced by [   ] cubes.

The [   ] is balanced by [   ] cubes.

You need:
● cubes
● balance
● objects to balance

The **heavier** object is the [   ] .

It is [   ] cubes heavier

than the [   ] .

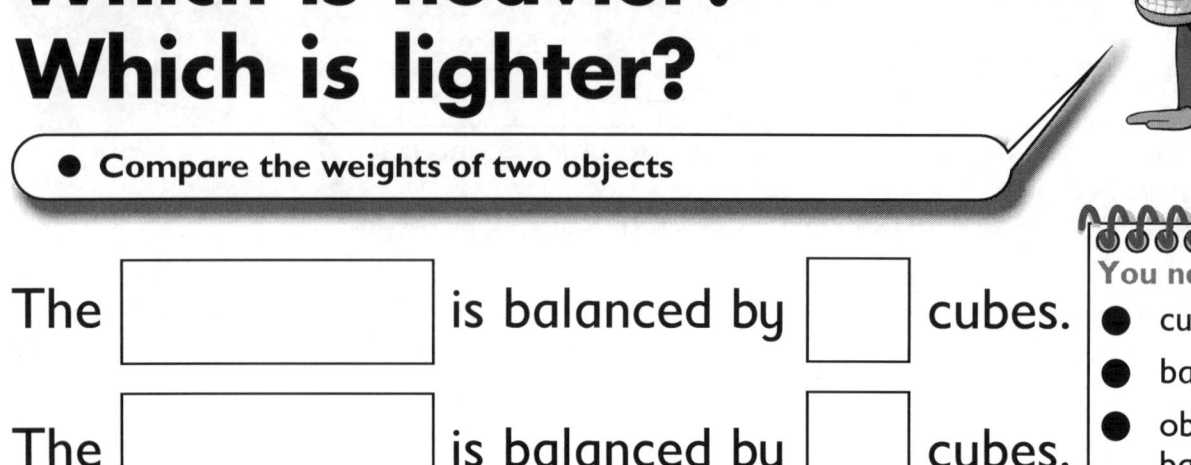

_____

The [   ] is balanced by [   ] cubes.

The [   ] is balanced by [   ] cubes.

The **lighter** object is the [   ] .

It is [   ] cubes lighter

than the [   ] .

Teacher's notes
Balance an object with cubes. Write the result. Then, find another object and
balance it with cubes. Write the result. Next, compare the two results to decide
which object is heavier/lighter and by how many cubes.

Name _____ Date _____

Stamp charts

You need:
● coloured pencils

● **Draw diagrams to show what was found**

stamp pictures

Number

| bird | fish | flower | building |

Picture

stamp shapes

square	
rectangle	
triangle	

☐ **stands for one stamp**

stamp	number
bird	
fish	
flower	
building	

stamp	number
square	
rectangle	
triangle	

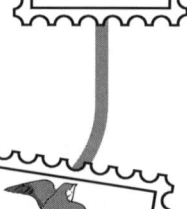

Teacher's notes
Top section: Colour a square in the block graph for each stamp.
Middle section: Choose a shape to stand for one stamp in the pictogram. Draw one shape for each stamp.
Bottom section: Complete the tables.

83

Name _____ Date _____

School race

● **Show what happened using lists**

All runners	Girls' race	Boys' race
1. Bob	1. Amy	1. Bob
2. _____	2. _____	2. _____
3. _____	3. _____	3. _____
4. _____	4. _____	4. _____
5. _____	5. _____	5. _____
6. _____	6. _____	6. _____
7. _____	7. _____	7. _____
8. _____		8. _____
9. _____		
10. _____		
11. _____		
12. _____		
13. _____		
14. _____		
15. _____		

Teacher's notes
Complete the results score-boards for all the runners, for all the
boys in the race and all the girls in the race.

Name _____ Date _____

It's half past what?

● **Read the time to the half hour**

half past __2__

half past _____

half past _____

half past _____

half past _____

half past _____

half past 11

half past 7

half past 3

half past 4

half past 12

half past 8

Teacher's notes
Top section: Look carefully at each clock. Then write the time in the space below.
Bottom section: Read the time under each clock. Then draw the hands in their correct positions.

Name _____ Date _____

Time dice

You need:
● 1–12 dice
● blank 1–6 dice with labels

● **Read the time to the hour and half hour**

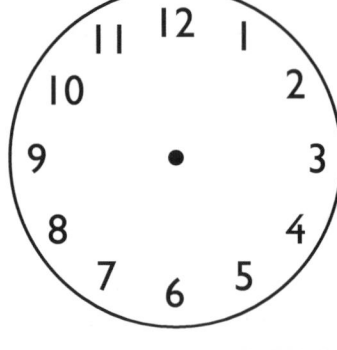

Teacher's notes
Take a 1-12 dice and a blank dice with one of the following labels on each side: o'clock, o'clock, o'clock, half past, half past, half past. Roll both the dice together, drawing the resulting time in a clock face and writing the time underneath. Repeat for all the clock faces on the sheet.

Name _____ Date _____

Rock pool positions

You need:
- scissors ● glue

● **Use words to describe position, direction and movement**

Teacher's notes
Top section: Look at what each character finds in the rock pools.
Middle section: Trace over each character's route on the grid.
Bottom section: Cut out the arrows and stick them on the spaces provided.

Name _____ Date _____

Change from 15p

You need:
● scissors ● glue

● **Solve problems about money**

 Cavan has 15p
He buys  6p

$\boxed{15}$ p $-$ $\boxed{6}$ p $=$ $\boxed{}$ p

 Thea has 15p
She buys 7p

$\boxed{}$ p $-$ $\boxed{}$ p $=$ $\boxed{}$ p

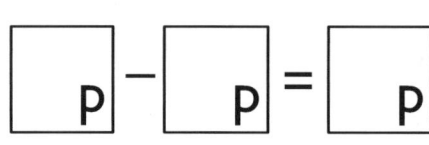

 Kaya has 15p
She buys 8p

$\boxed{}$ p $-$ $\boxed{}$ p $=$ $\boxed{}$ p

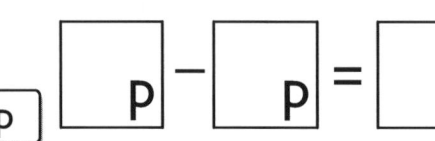

 Charlie has 15p
He buys 9p

$\boxed{}$ p $-$ $\boxed{}$ p $=$ $\boxed{}$ p

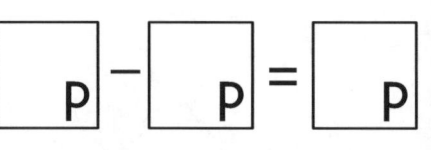

Teacher's notes
Each character has 15p to spend. Use the row of pennies to work out how much change they will get and write the subtraction calculation in the space provided. Then cut out the coins from the bottom of the sheet, identifying the correct amount of change for each child before sticking them into place.

Name _____ Date _____

Match that time!

You need:
● scissors

● **Read the time to the hour or half hour**

half past 8	10 o'clock	half past 11
half past 4	6 o'clock	3 o'clock
half past 12	1 o'clock	half past 2

Teacher's notes
Cut out both sets of cards. Mix them up and spread them out face down. Then, playing in pairs, take
turns to turn over any two cards. If they match, keep them. If they do not, return them face down.
Carry on until all the cards have been matched. The player with the most cards is the winner.

Name _____ Date _____

O'clock times

● **Read the time to the hour**

5 o'clock

12 o'clock

10 o'clock

4 o'clock

 **after** **one** **hour** →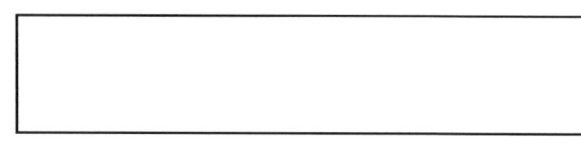

 **after** **one** **hour** →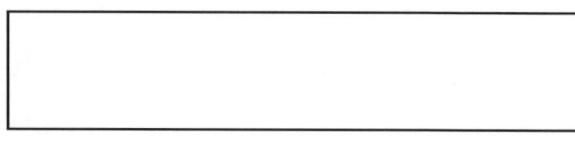

 **after** **one** **hour** →

Teacher's notes
Top section: Draw the time on the clock face to show when the activity happens.
Bottom section: Draw the time on the clock face after one hour. Write this time next to the clock face.

Name _____ Date _____

Draw this!

You need:
- scissors

● Use words to describe position and direction

91

Teacher's notes
Working in pairs, the children cut out the grids from the sheet, so that they will have one with designs and one without. Each takes it in turn to describe their patterned grid to the other, who then draws onto their blank grid to create one the same. Once complete, they compare the original with the copy, before reversing roles.

Name _____ Date _____

What can I buy with 15p?

● **Solve problems about money**

Theo buys   ☐ p + ☐ p = 15p

Ben buys   ☐ p + ☐ p = 15p

Sara buys   ☐ p + ☐ p = 15p

8p	10p	9p	6p	5p	7p
	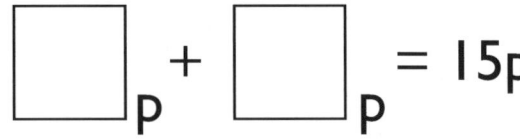			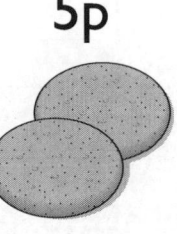	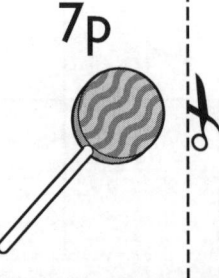

Teacher's notes
Each person has spent 15p exactly. Cut out the items from the bottom of the sheet and pair them so that each pair totals 15p. Give each character a pair of items and glue them in place.

Name _____ Date _____

Patterns of fives

You need:
- scissors
- glue

- Count on or back in ones, twos, fives or tens and know the multiples of 2, 5 and 10

0		10	15	20
30	25		15	10
5	10	15	20	
20	15		5	0
30	25	20		10
10	15	20	25	

 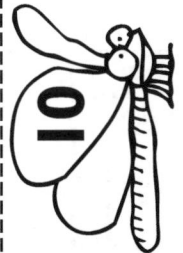    

20   10   30   5   15   25

Teacher's notes

Cut out the bugs from the bottom of the sheet. Look at each row in the bug parade and, counting in fives, position each one in the correct place in the row.

Name _____ Date _____

House numbers

● **Count on in twos and recognise odd and even numbers**

These are the houses with **even** numbers.

These are the houses with **odd** numbers.

94

Teacher's notes
Top section: Count on in steps of two from two. Identify and colour the even numbers. Then write the numbers in the row of even houses. *Bottom section:* Count on in steps of two from one. Identify and colour the odd numbers, then write the numbers in the row of odd houses.

Name _____ Date _____

Double deckers

You need:
● scissors ● glue

● **Know doubles of numbers to 10**

0 1 2 3 4 5 6 7 8 9 10 11 12 13 14 15 16 17 18 19 20

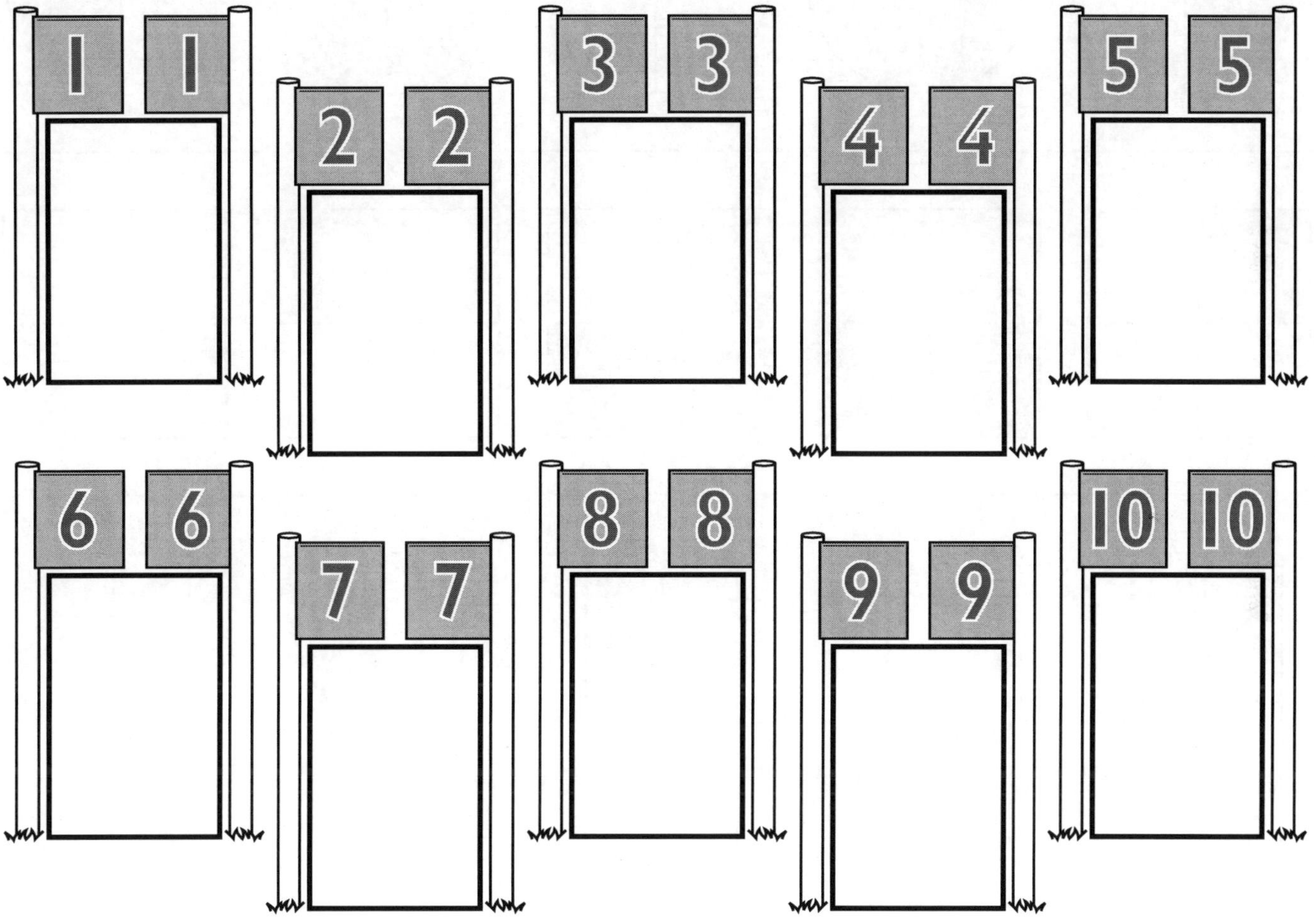

1 1

2 2

3 3

4 4

5 5

6 6

7 7

8 8

9 9

10 10

8   16   6   18   2

12   4   20   10   14

Teacher's notes
Cut out the buses from the bottom of the sheet. Look at the bus stops and match them to the bus showing their addition double. Use the passenger number track to help.

Name _____ Date _____

Quarter questions

You need:
● coloured pencils

● **Recognise a quarter of a shape**

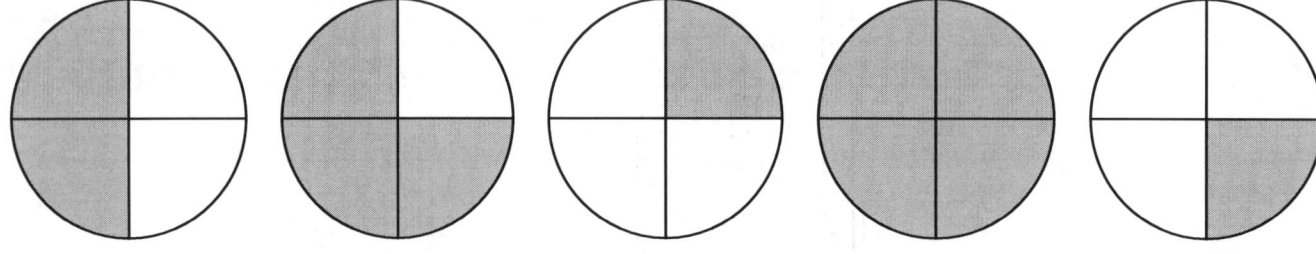

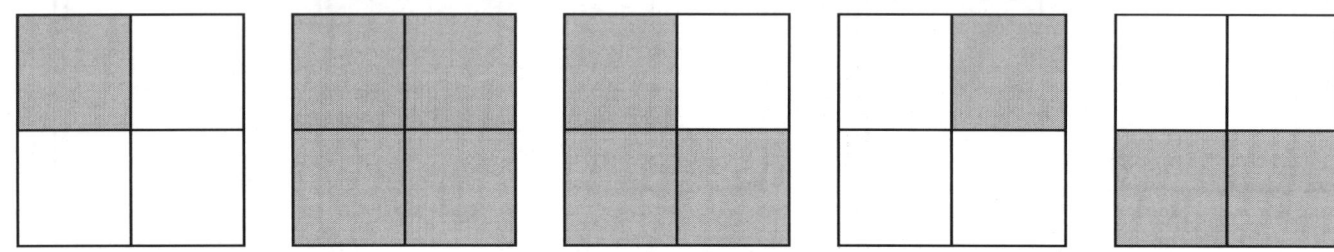

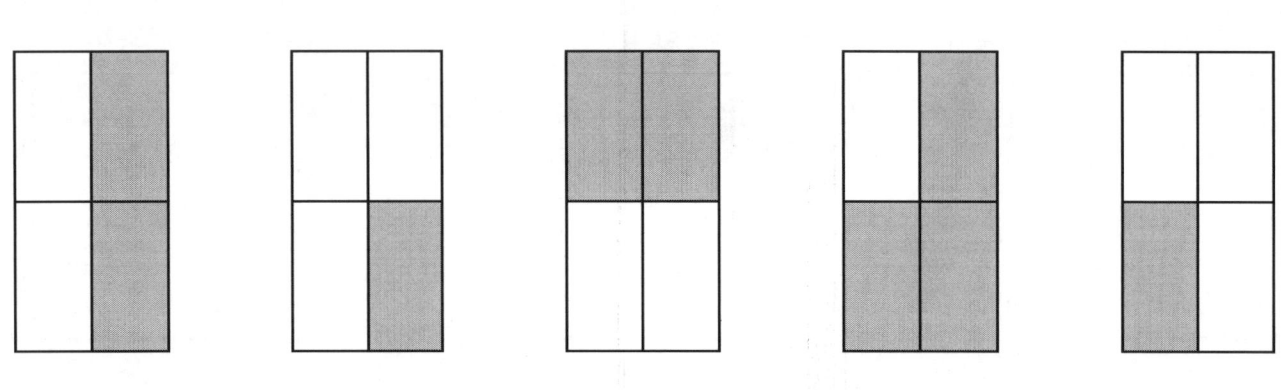

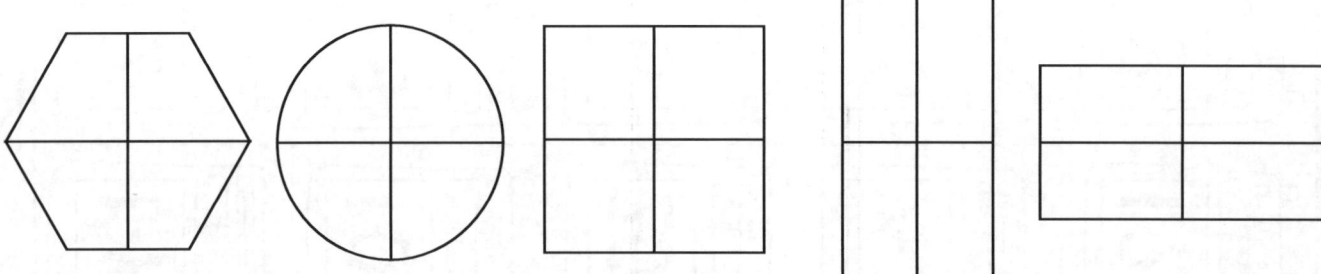

Teacher's notes

Top section: Colour the shapes in each row where one quarter is shaded.
Bottom section: Colour each quarter of the shapes a different colour.

Name _____ Date _____

How many socks?

● Solve problems combining groups of 2

| 1 | pair has |
| 2 | socks |

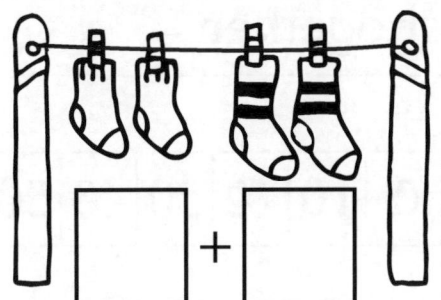

[ ] + [ ]

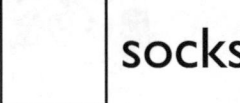

| | pairs have |
| | socks |

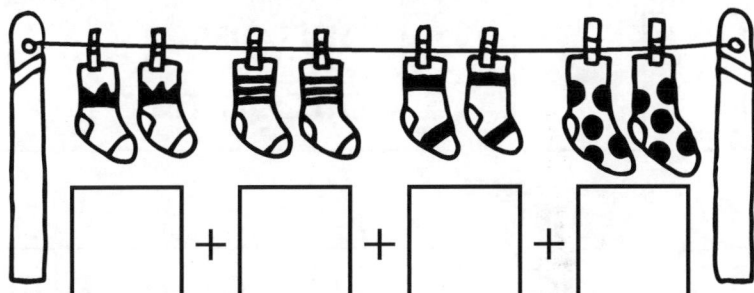

[ ] + [ ] + [ ] + [ ]

| | pairs have |
| | socks |

[ ] + [ ] + [ ]

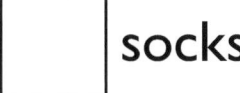

| | pairs have |
| | socks |

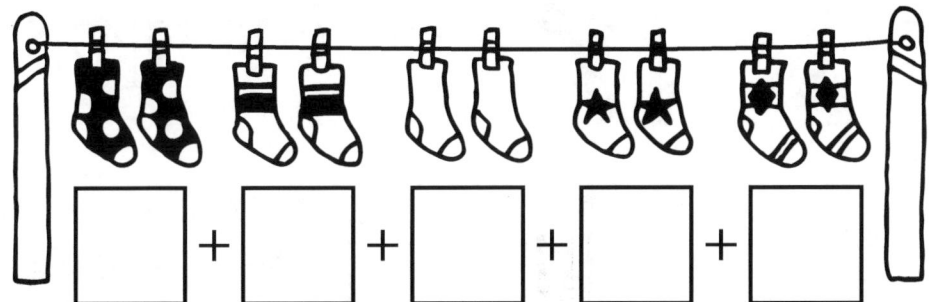

[ ] + [ ] + [ ] + [ ] + [ ]

| | pairs have |
| | socks |

Teacher's notes
Find out how many socks there are on each washing line by writing each calculation
as a repeated addition. Then complete the sentences.

Name _____ Date _____

Button boxes

- Solve problems combining groups of 10

 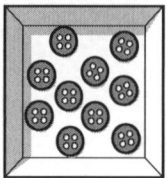

0	10	20	30	40	50

$\boxed{10}$ + $\boxed{10}$ ➡ $\boxed{}$ buttons altogether

 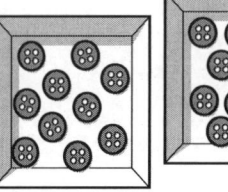

0	10	20	30	40	50

$\boxed{}$ + $\boxed{}$ + $\boxed{}$ ➡ $\boxed{}$ buttons altogether

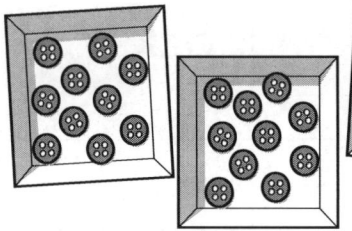  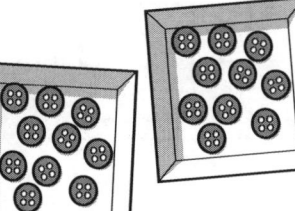

0	10	20	30	40	50

$\boxed{}$ + $\boxed{}$ + $\boxed{}$ + $\boxed{}$ + $\boxed{}$ ➡ $\boxed{}$ buttons altogether

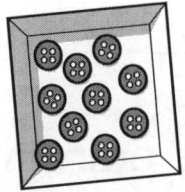 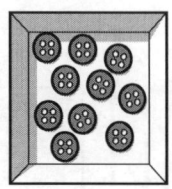 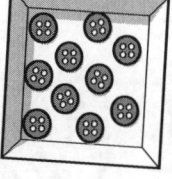 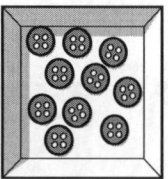

0	10	20	30	40	50

$\boxed{}$ + $\boxed{}$ + $\boxed{}$ + $\boxed{}$ ➡ $\boxed{}$ buttons altogether

Teacher's notes
Each box has 10 buttons inside. Use the 10s number tracks to work out how many buttons there are altogether in each set of boxes. Show the jumps on the track then write the answer as a repeated addition calculation in the spaces provided.

Name _____ Date _____

Patterns of tens

You need:
● scissors ● glue

● **Count on or back in tens**

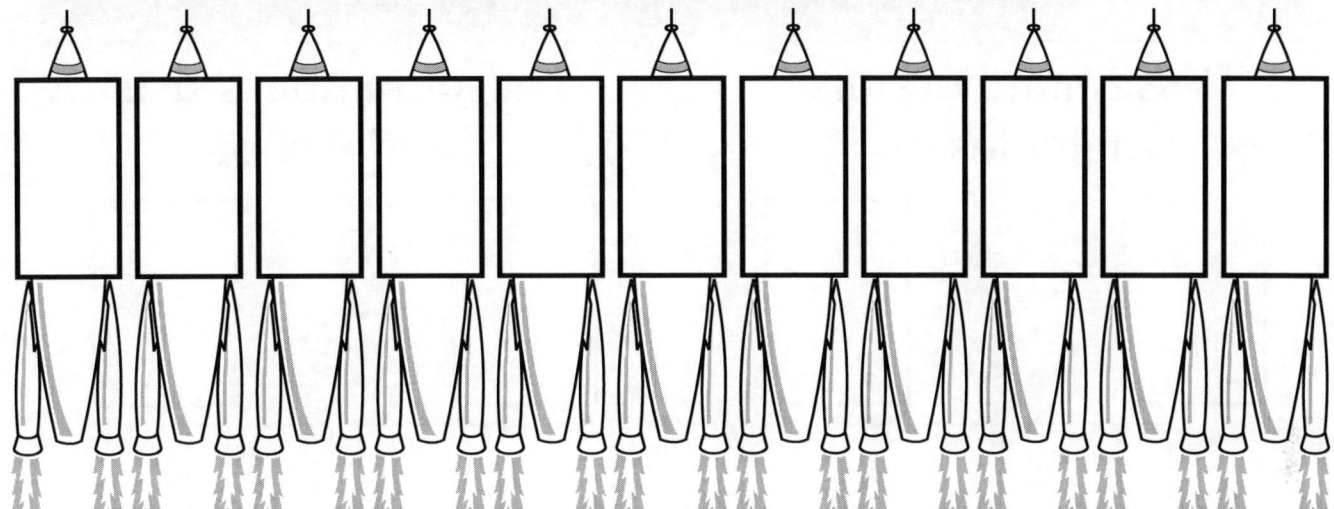

20 30 ☐ ☐ ☐ ☐

90 80 ☐ ☐ ☐ ☐

50 60 ☐ ☐ ☐ ☐

40 60 10 50 0 30 100 90 20 70 80

Teacher's notes
Cut out the multiples of 10 from the bottom of the sheet and arrange them in order from 0–100. In each row underneath, complete the sequence by counting on or back in 10s and write the missing numbers in the spaces provided.

Name _____ Date _____

Mixed up multiples

You need:
● scissors ● glue

● Count on or back in twos, fives or tens and know the multiples of 2, 5 and 10

These numbers are multiples of

These numbers are multiples of

These numbers are multiples of

These numbers are multiples of

70 10 35 100 14 40 50 8 ✂

Teacher's notes
Cut out the numbers from the bottom of the sheet and sort them into the correct sets. Then write another two multiples into each set.

100

Name _____ Date _____

Collector's corner

● **Solve word problems**

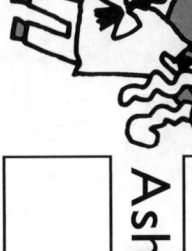

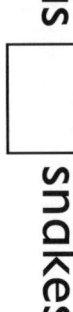

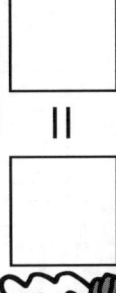

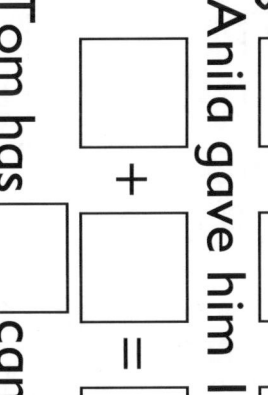

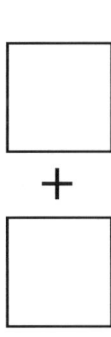
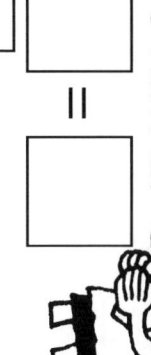
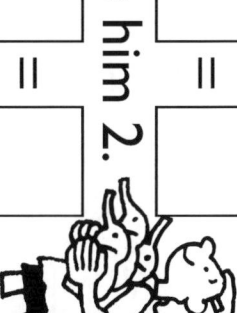

Georgia had 6 giraffes. Naomi gave her 1. Saeed gave her 2 more.

☐ + ☐ = ☐

☐ + ☐ = ☐

Now Georgia has ☐ giraffes.

Sunita had 7 snakes. Kimoko gave her 2 more. Asha gave her 2.

☐ + ☐ = ☐

☐ + ☐ = ☐

Now Sunita has ☐ snakes.

Ellis had 5 elephants. Lily gave him 3 more. Tom gave him 2.

☐ + ☐ = ☐

☐ + ☐ = ☐

Now Ellis has ☐ elephants.

Tom had 8 camels. Deepak gave him 3 more. Anila gave him 1 more.

☐ + ☐ = ☐

☐ + ☐ = ☐

Now Tom has ☐ camels.

Teacher's notes
In each panel, work out the first problem and write the calculation in the first row of boxes.
Now use the answer to the first problem to work out the second problem. Write the
calculation in the second row of boxes. Then write the final answer in the last box.

Name _____ Date _____

Quarter questions

You need:
● coloured pencil

● **Find one quarter of a group of objects**

$\frac{1}{4}$ of ☐ is ☐

$\frac{1}{4}$ of ☐ is ☐

$\frac{1}{4}$ of ☐ is ☐

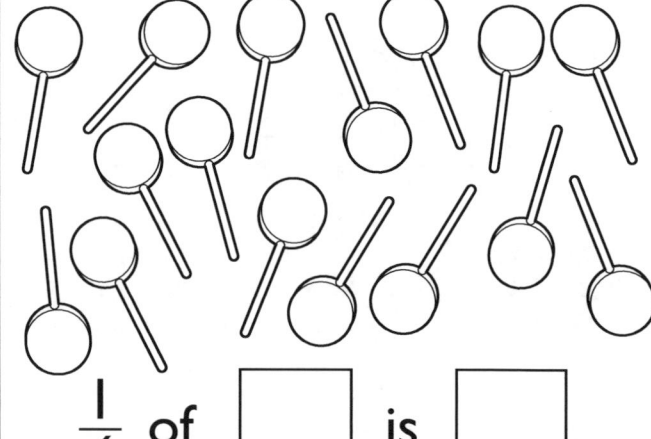

$\frac{1}{4}$ of ☐ is ☐

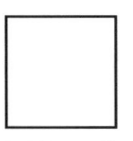

$\frac{1}{4}$ of ☐ is ☐

$\frac{1}{4}$ of ☐ is ☐

Teacher's notes
Count the number of objects in each set and colour one quarter in each one.

Name _____ Date _____

Money box fives

- Solve problems combining groups of 5

☐ + ☐ + ☐

➡ ☐ pennies altogether

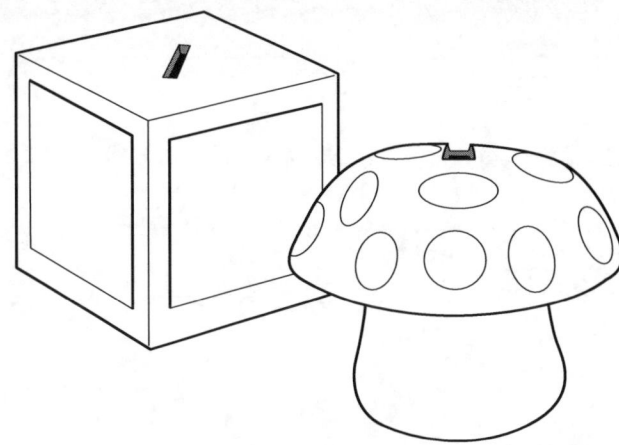

☐ + ☐

➡ ☐ pennies altogether

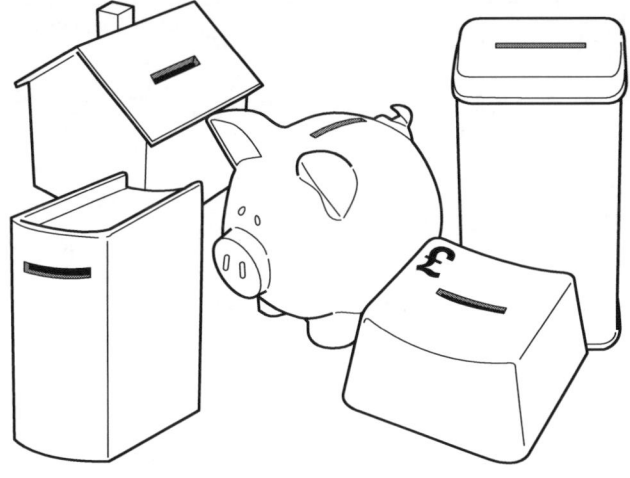

☐ + ☐ + ☐ + ☐ + ☐

➡ ☐ pennies altogether

☐ + ☐ + ☐ + ☐

➡ ☐ pennies altogether

© HarperCollins Publishers Ltd 2008

Teacher's notes
There are five pennies in each money box. Look at each group of money boxes and
work out the total amount of money for each group. Write each calculation as a
repeated addition.

103

Name _____ Date _____

Share the sheep!

You need:
● coloured pencils

● **Solve problems involving sharing into equal groups**

3 groups

☐ sheep in each group.

4 groups

☐ sheep in each group.

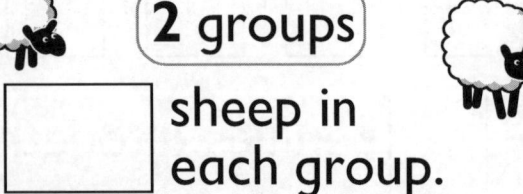

2 groups

☐ sheep in each group.

4 groups

☐ sheep in each group.

Teacher's notes

The farmer is sorting each field of sheep into groups. Look at the number of sheep in each field and then share them into the number of groups written underneath by colouring each set in a different colour. Complete each sentence underneath.

Name _____ Date _____

Countryside counting

● Read, write and order numbers to at least 20

10 · 11 · ☐ · ☐ · ☐ · 15

8 · ☐ · 10 · ☐ · 12 · ☐

14 · 15 · ☐ · ☐ · 18 · ☐

16 · 15 · ☐ · 13 · ☐ · ☐

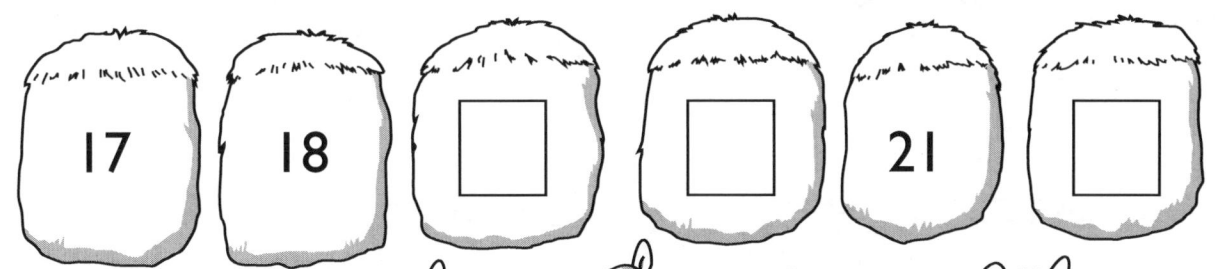

17 · 18 · ☐ · ☐ · 21 · ☐

25 · 24 · ☐ · 22 · ☐ · 20

Teacher's notes
Look at the number sequences and complete each one. Write the missing numbers in the spaces provided.

© HarperCollinsPublishers Ltd 2008

105

Name _____ Date _____

Washing line numbers

You need:
● scissors

● **Say the number that is 10 more or less**

10 less? | 13 | 10 more?

10 less? | 18 | 10 more?

10 less? | 20 | 10 more?

10 less? | 23 | 10 more?

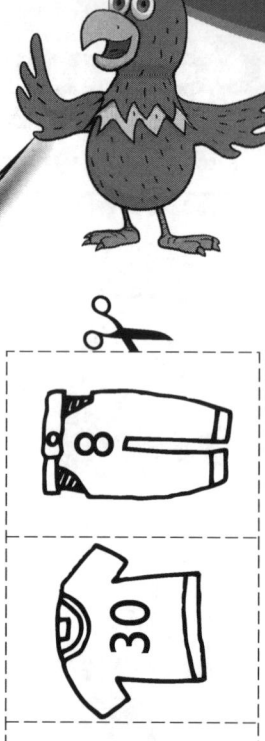

8

30

13

28

3

33

10

23

Teacher's notes
Cut out the pictures of clothes on the right-hand side and sort them into sets to match the numbered item on each washing line. Stick on the left-hand side of the number line the number which is ten less than the number on the line, and on the right-hand side of the line the number which is ten more.

Name _____ Date _____

Jump and add

You need:
- red and blue coloured pencils

- **Know that addition can be done in any order**

1

| 2 | 6 |

$$2 + 1 + 6 = 9$$

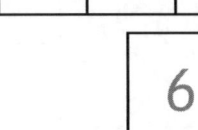

| 0 | 1 | 2 | 3 | 4 | 5 | 6 | 7 | 8 | 9 | 10 |

$$6 + 2 + 1 = 9$$

2

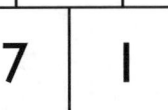

| 7 | 1 |

$$\square + \square + \square = \square$$

| 0 | 1 | 2 | 3 | 4 | 5 | 6 | 7 | 8 | 9 | 10 |

$$\square + \square + \square = \square$$

3

| 3 | 4 |

$$\square + \square + \square = \square$$

| 0 | 1 | 2 | 3 | 4 | 5 | 6 | 7 | 8 | 9 | 10 |

$$\square + \square + \square = \square$$

1

| 4 | 3 |

$$\square + \square + \square = \square$$

| 0 | 1 | 2 | 3 | 4 | 5 | 6 | 7 | 8 | 9 | 10 |

$$\square + \square + \square = \square$$

Teacher's notes
Look at each set of numbers on the left. Write them down in any order in the boxes above the number line. Complete the calculation and also show it (in red) as 'jumps' along the number line. Now write the numbers in a different order in the boxes below the number line and repeat the process (using blue).

107

Name _____ Date _____

Make patterns with 8

You need:
● coloured pencils

● **Recognise patterns in number sentences**

1	+	7	= 8		
	+		= 8		
	+		= 8		
	+		= 8		
	+		= 8		
	+		= 8		

8 –	1	=	7	
8 –		=		
8 –		=		
8 –		=		
8 –		=		
8 –		=		

108

Teacher's notes
Top section: Colour one pear at a time and record in each row of boxes the combination of coloured and uncoloured pears.
Bottom section: Repeat the procedure with the oranges, crossing out the coloured oranges.

Name _____ Date _____

Tens and units tents

You need:
● scissors ● glue

● Understand the value of the digits in a two-digit number

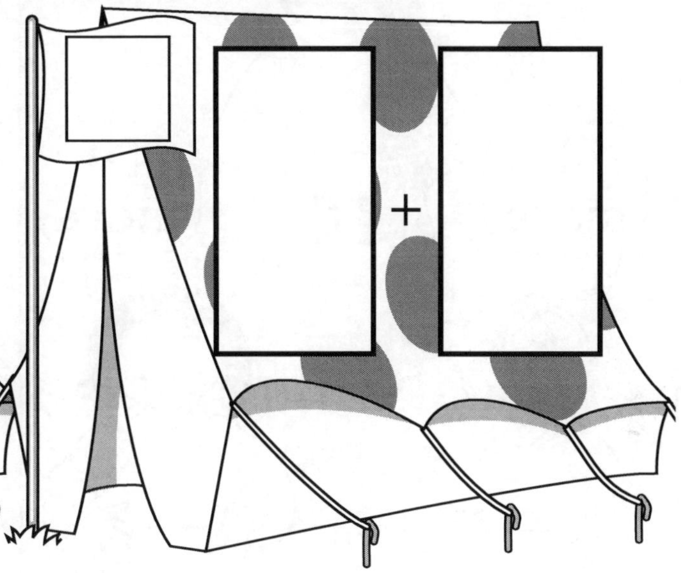

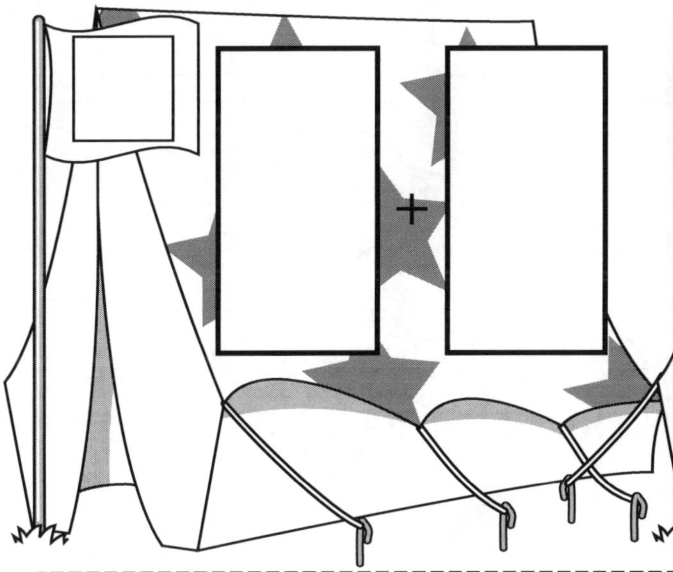

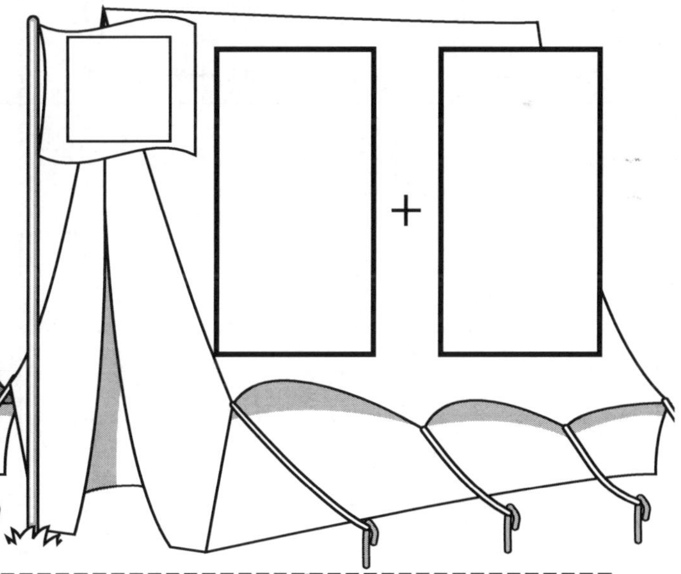

Teacher's notes

Cut out the children from the bottom of the sheet. Match a pair of children to each tent to find out the number of their pitch. Write the number on each flag.

Name _____ Date _____

More or less?

- **Say the number that is 1 or 10 more or less**

1 more **10** **10 more**	**1 less** **14** **10 more**
10 more **27** **1 more**	**1 less** **35** **10 more**

Teacher's notes
Look at the number shown with each group of children. Read the instruction spoken
by each child and write the correct number in the corresponding space.

Name _____ Date _____

Adding tens

You need:
● coloured pencils

● Add 10 or 20 to a number

| 7 | 8 | 9 | 10 | 11 | 12 | 13 | 14 | 15 | 16 | 17 | 18 | 19 | 20 | 21 | 22 | 23 | 24 | 25 | 26 | 27 | 28 | 29 | 30 |

Add on 10.

$\boxed{7}$ + $\boxed{10}$ = $\boxed{17}$

Add on 20.

$\boxed{7}$ + $\boxed{20}$ = $\boxed{}$

| 11 | 12 | 13 | 14 | 15 | 16 | 17 | 18 | 19 | 20 | 21 | 22 | 23 | 24 | 25 | 26 | 27 | 28 | 29 | 30 | 31 | 32 | 33 | 34 |

Add on 10.

$\boxed{}$ + $\boxed{}$ = $\boxed{}$

Add on 20.

$\boxed{}$ + $\boxed{}$ = $\boxed{}$

| 16 | 17 | 18 | 19 | 20 | 21 | 22 | 23 | 24 | 25 | 26 | 27 | 28 | 29 | 30 | 31 | 32 | 33 | 34 | 35 | 36 | 37 | 38 | 39 |

Add on 10.

$\boxed{}$ + $\boxed{}$ = $\boxed{}$

Add on 20.

$\boxed{}$ + $\boxed{}$ = $\boxed{}$

| 24 | 25 | 26 | 27 | 28 | 29 | 30 | 31 | 32 | 33 | 34 | 35 | 36 | 37 | 38 | 39 | 40 | 41 | 42 | 43 | 44 | 45 | 46 | 47 |

Add on 10.

$\boxed{}$ + $\boxed{}$ = $\boxed{}$

Add on 20.

$\boxed{}$ + $\boxed{}$ = $\boxed{}$

| 38 | 39 | 40 | 41 | 42 | 43 | 44 | 45 | 46 | 47 | 48 | 49 | 50 | 51 | 52 | 53 | 54 | 55 | 56 | 57 | 58 | 59 | 60 | 61 |

Add on 10.

$\boxed{}$ + $\boxed{}$ = $\boxed{}$

Add on 20.

$\boxed{}$ + $\boxed{}$ = $\boxed{}$

Teacher's notes
Follow the instructions on each section of the number track to add on 10 then 20 to
the number at the start of each track. Complete each addition calculation underneath
the number tracks.

Name _____ Date _____

Taking tens

You need:
- coloured pencils

● **Subtract 10 or 20 from a number**

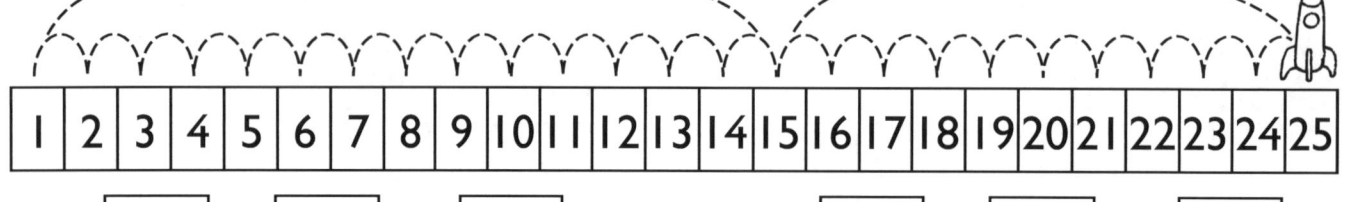

| 1 | 2 | 3 | 4 | 5 | 6 | 7 | 8 | 9 | 10 | 11 | 12 | 13 | 14 | 15 | 16 | 17 | 18 | 19 | 20 | 21 | 22 | 23 | 24 | 25 |

$\boxed{25} - \boxed{10} = \boxed{}$ $\boxed{25} - \boxed{20} = \boxed{}$

| 6 | 7 | 8 | 9 | 10 | 11 | 12 | 13 | 14 | 15 | 16 | 17 | 18 | 19 | 20 | 21 | 22 | 23 | 24 | 25 | 26 | 27 | 28 | 29 | 30 |

$\boxed{} - \boxed{10} = \boxed{}$ $\boxed{} - \boxed{20} = \boxed{}$

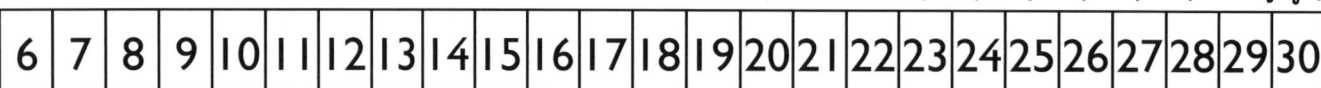

| 14 | 15 | 16 | 17 | 18 | 19 | 20 | 21 | 22 | 23 | 24 | 25 | 26 | 27 | 28 | 29 | 30 | 31 | 32 | 33 | 34 | 35 | 36 | 37 | 38 |

$\boxed{} - \boxed{10} = \boxed{}$ $\boxed{} - \boxed{20} = \boxed{}$

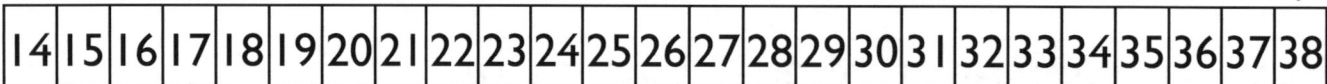

| 19 | 20 | 21 | 22 | 23 | 24 | 25 | 26 | 27 | 28 | 29 | 30 | 31 | 32 | 33 | 34 | 35 | 36 | 37 | 38 | 39 | 40 | 41 | 42 | 43 |

$\boxed{} - \boxed{10} = \boxed{}$ $\boxed{} - \boxed{20} = \boxed{}$

Teacher's notes
Look at the number that the spaceship is taking off from. Take away 10, colour the number on the track and write this as a subtraction calculation. Then take off 20, colour the number on the track and then write this as a subtraction calculation.

Name _____ Date _____

Solid shape sequences

You need:
● scissors ● glue

● **Continue patterns involving shapes**

 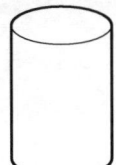 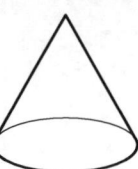  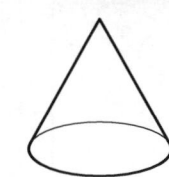 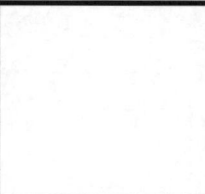

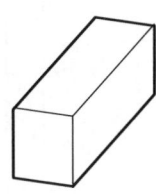 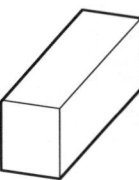    

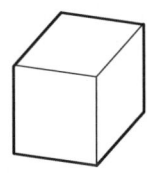 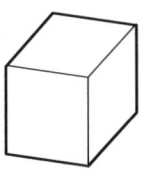    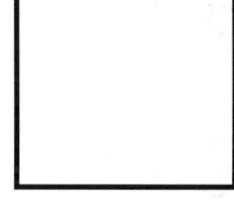

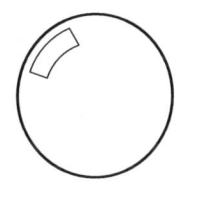     

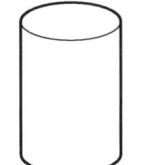 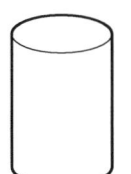 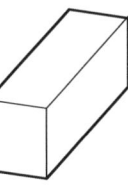 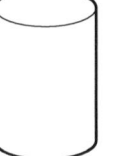 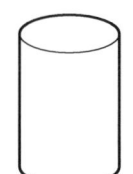 

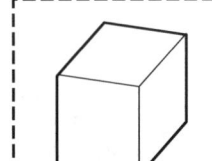 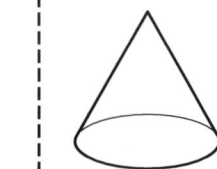 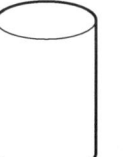 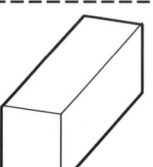 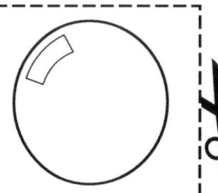

Teacher's notes
Look at each pattern. Cut out the shapes from the bottom of the sheet and choose
one to complete each solid shape pattern correctly.

Name _____ Date _____

Solid shape sweet sorter

You need:
● scissors ● glue

● **Recognise features of 3-D shapes**

curved edges	straight edges	no edges

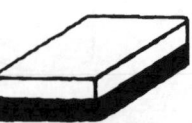

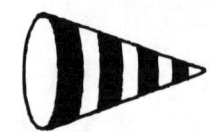

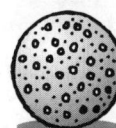

Teacher's notes
Cut out the sweets from the bottom of the sheet and stick them onto the appropriate package, according to the label on each of the four boxes.

Name _____ Date _____

Counting on the moon

You need:
- red coloured pencils

- **Add two numbers**

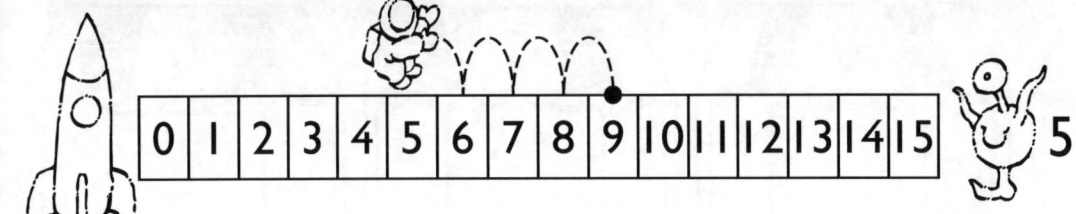

5 + 4 = ☐

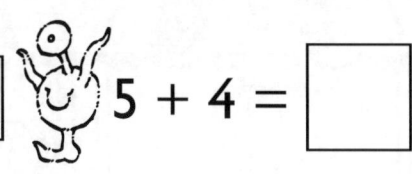

7 + 3 = ☐

8 + 4 = ☐

9 + 5 = ☐

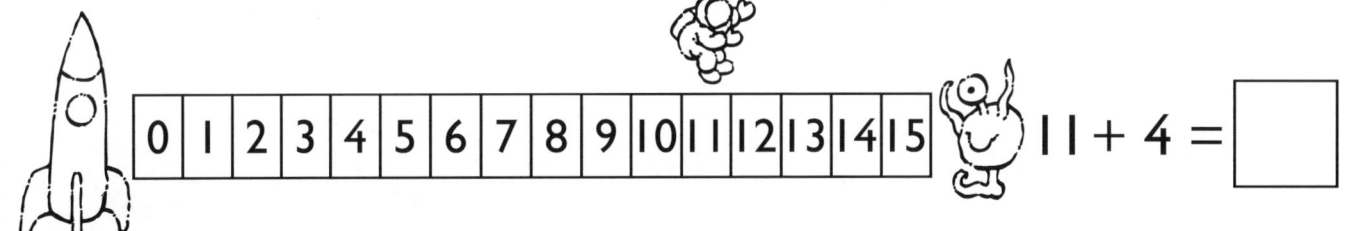

11 + 4 = ☐

Teacher's notes

Find the answer to each addition calculation by making the astronaut jump along the number track towards the alien. Remember to start from the larger number in the calculation and show the jumps, colouring the answer on the track in red.

Name _____ Date _____

Market stalls make 7

You need:
● scissors ● glue

● **Know addition facts for 7**

| 2 | 6 | 5 | 0 |

2 + 5

[ ] + [ ]   [ ] + [ ]   [ ] + [ ]

| 4 | 1 | 7 | 3 |

[ ] + [ ]   [ ] + [ ]   [ ] + [ ]   [ ] + [ ]

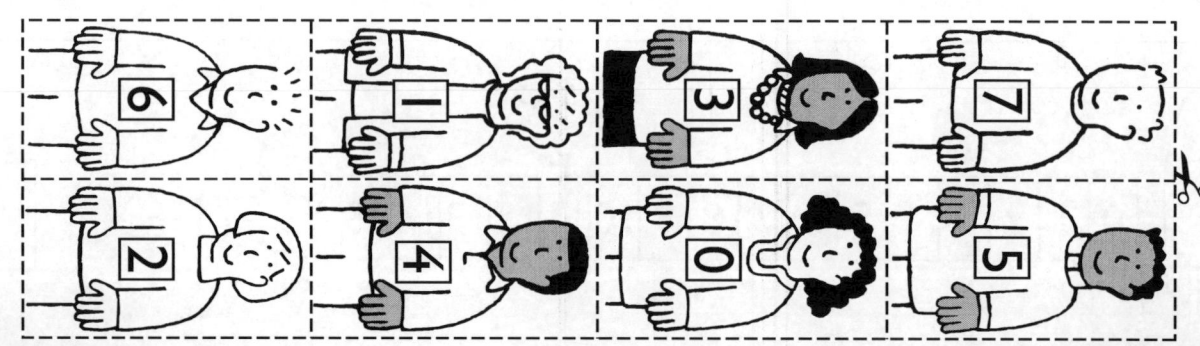

116

Teacher's notes
Cut out the pictures of the people in the bottom section. Then match each person to a market stall so that the total of their two numbers is seven. Write in the boxes the resulting addition fact for seven.

Name _____ Date _____

Passenger doubles

● **Know doubles of numbers to at least 10**

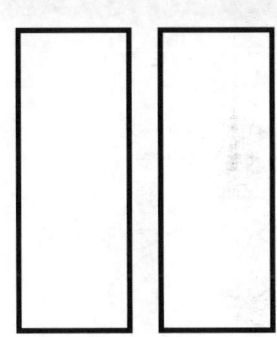

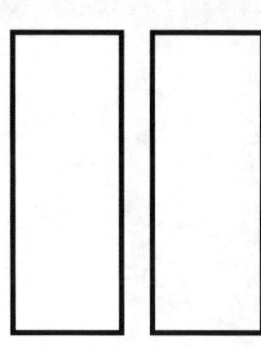

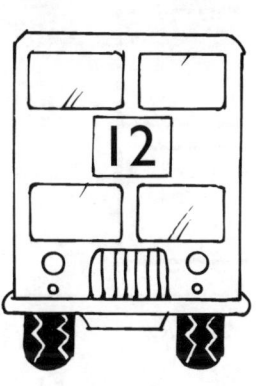
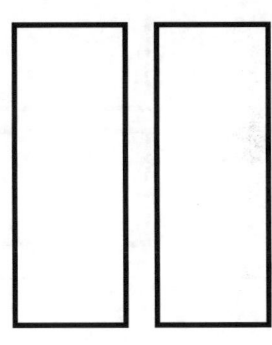

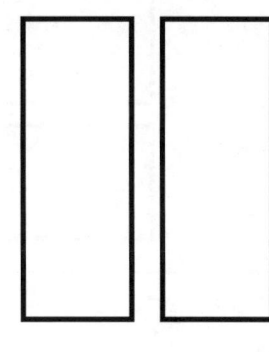

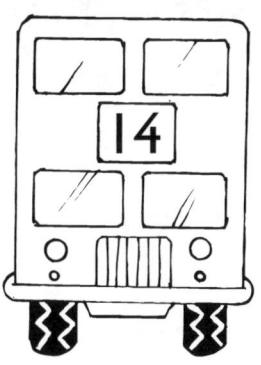
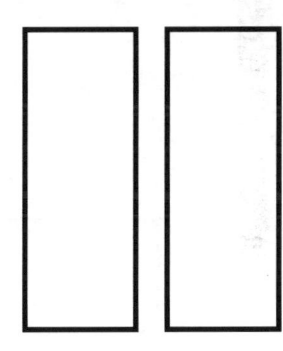

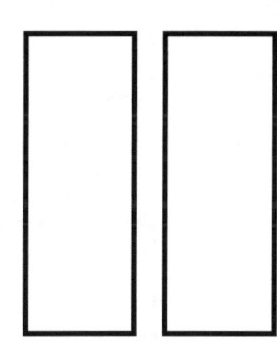

Teacher's notes
Cut out the pictures of the characters from the bottom of the sheet. Then match them
to each other according to their numbers. Next, match each pair of numbers to the bus
which shows their total and stick the two characters alongside that bus.

117

Name _____ Date _____

Add two ways

● **Know that addition can be done in any order**

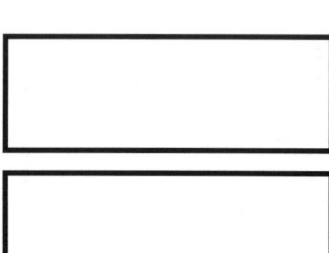

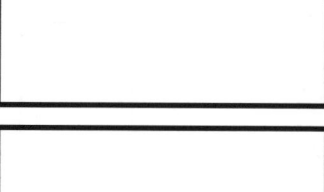

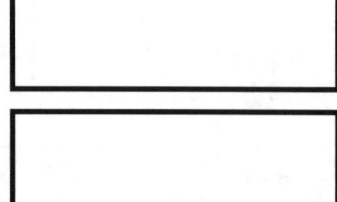

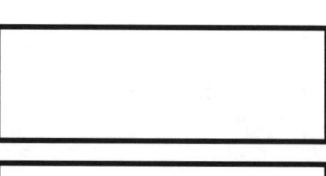

| 5 + 4 = ☐ | 4 + 8 = ☐ | 4 + 7 = ☐ | 4 + 5 = ☐ |
| 6 + 8 = ☐ | 7 + 4 = ☐ | 8 + 6 = ☐ | 8 + 4 = ☐ |

Teacher's notes
Look carefully at each picture. Then cut out and stick below each picture the correct addition calculations. In each pair of calculations, colour the one that has the larger number first.

Name _____ Date _____

Continuing carpets

You need:
● scissors ● glue

● **Continue patterns involving shapes**

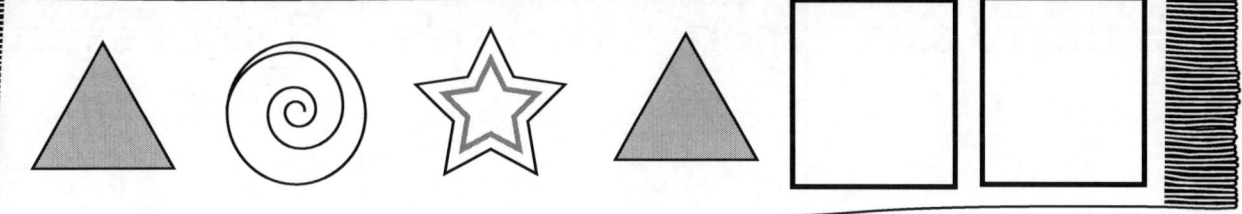

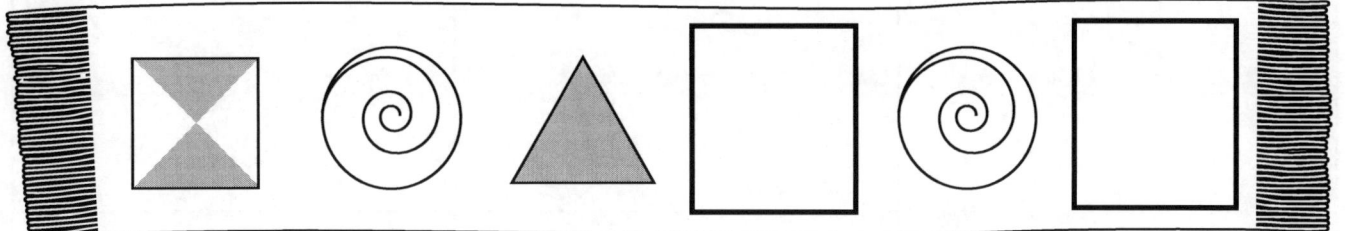

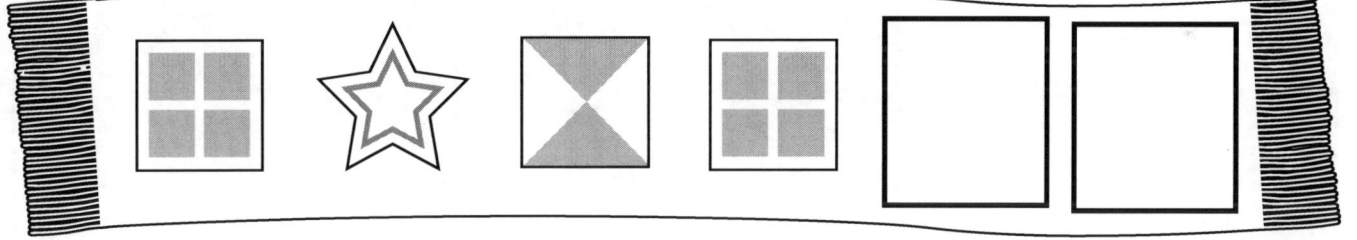

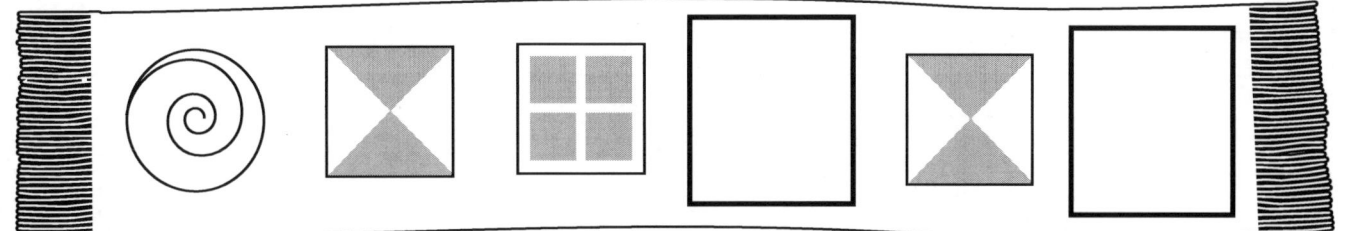

Teacher's notes

Look at each carpet pattern using three shapes. Cut out the shapes from the bottom of the sheet and stick each one into the correct space on the carpets to complete the patterns.

Name _____ Date _____

Sorting shapes

You need:
- scissors
- glue

● **Know features of 2-D shapes**

less than 3 sides	more than 3 sides	3 sides exactly
curved sides only	**straight sides only**	**curved and straight sides**

Teacher's notes
Cut out the shapes from the bottom of the sheet. Sort the striped shapes into the top sets and the spotted shapes into the sets underneath. Stick them into the correct place.

Name _____ Date _____

What's the difference?

You need:
● coloured pencils

● Understand subtraction as 'finding the difference'

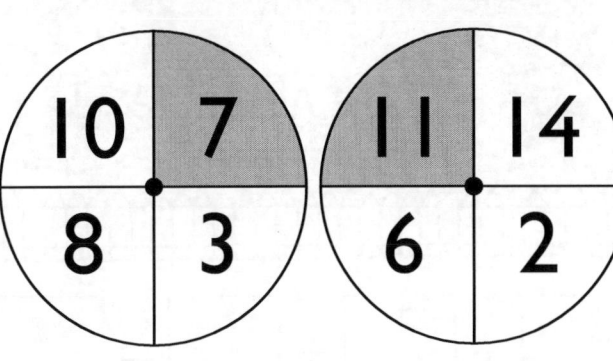

10	7
8	3

11	14
6	2

| 11 | (−) | 7 | (=) | 4 |

| 7 | (+) | 4 | (=) | 11 |

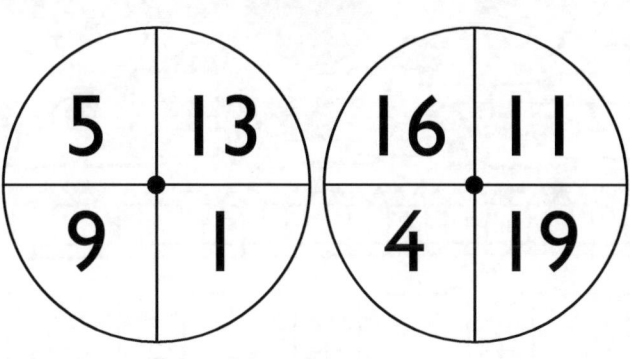

5	13
9	1

16	11
4	19

☐ ○ ☐ ○ ☐

☐ ○ ☐ ○ ☐

9	6
8	11

10	19
13	16

☐ ○ ☐ ○ ☐

☐ ○ ☐ ○ ☐

7	12
4	10

20	17
18	19

☐ ○ ☐ ○ ☐

☐ ○ ☐ ○ ☐

Teacher's notes

Look at each pair of spinners. Colour a number on each one and find the difference
between the two numbers you have chosen. Write them as a subtraction calculation
underneath. Can you write each as an addition calculation?

Name _____ Date _____

Tricky trios

You need:
● coloured pencils

● **Understand that addition can be done in any order**

$$\boxed{2} + \boxed{9} + \boxed{14} = \boxed{25}$$

$$\boxed{14} + \boxed{2} + \boxed{9} = \boxed{}$$

$$\boxed{} + \boxed{} + \boxed{} = \boxed{}$$

$$\boxed{} + \boxed{} + \boxed{} = \boxed{}$$

$$\boxed{} + \boxed{} + \boxed{} = \boxed{}$$

$$\boxed{} + \boxed{} + \boxed{} = \boxed{}$$

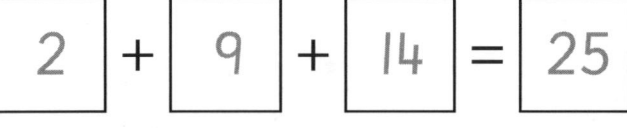

$$\boxed{} + \boxed{} + \boxed{} = \boxed{}$$

$$\boxed{} + \boxed{} + \boxed{} = \boxed{}$$

$$\boxed{} + \boxed{} + \boxed{} = \boxed{}$$

$$\boxed{} + \boxed{} + \boxed{} = \boxed{}$$

$$\boxed{} + \boxed{} + \boxed{} = \boxed{}$$

$$\boxed{} + \boxed{} + \boxed{} = \boxed{}$$

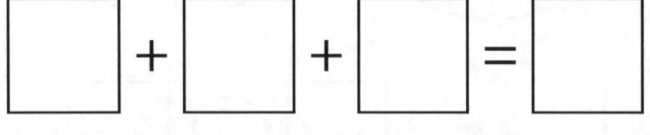

Teacher's notes

In each panel, look at the three numbers at the top and write them in the boxes
of the first addition calculation. Work out the answer using the number line to
help. Then rearrange the numbers (twice) and work out the answer.

Name _____ Date _____

Sail boat addition

- **Know and use doubles of numbers to at least 10**

8 + 8

6 + 6

7 + 8 =

6 + 7 =

3 + 4 =

4 + 4

3 + 3

4 + 5 =

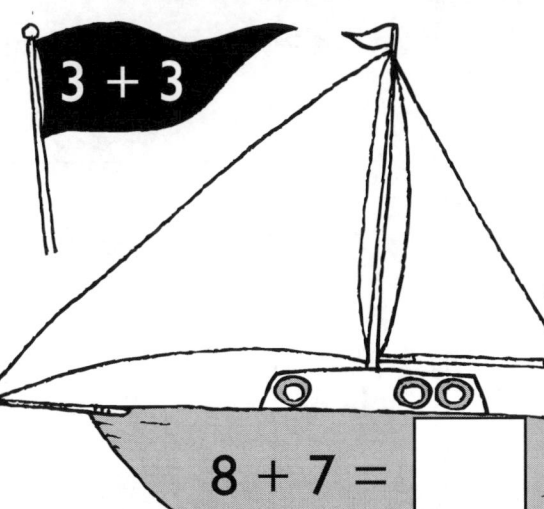

8 + 7 =

7 + 7

5 + 5

5 + 6 =

Teacher's notes
Work out the answer to each addition calculation using the 'doubles' number facts
flags to help you. Write your answers in the box provided.

Name ____________________ Date ____________

Playground addition

You need:

- coloured pencils

- **Know pairs of numbers that total 10**

3 + ☐ = 10

5 + ☐ = 10

9 + ☐ = 10

6 + ☐ = 10

8 + ☐ = 10

0 + ☐ = 10

4 + ☐ = 10

2 + ☐ = 10

7 + ☐ = 10

1 + ☐ = 10

10 + ☐ = 10

Teacher's notes

Complete each addition calculation showing totals for 10. As you find the missing number in each, colour the child showing the same missing number on their T-shirt.

Name _____ Date _____

Fill me up!

You need:
- scissors ● glue
- spare sheet of paper

● **Understand the language of capacity**

full	empty	almost full	almost empty

Teacher's notes
Cut out the labels and glue them onto a separate sheet of paper. Cut out each
container and sort it according to how much water it contains.

125

Name _____ Date _____

More than, less than containers

● **Understand the language of capacity**

a cup   a spoon

a bucket   a purse

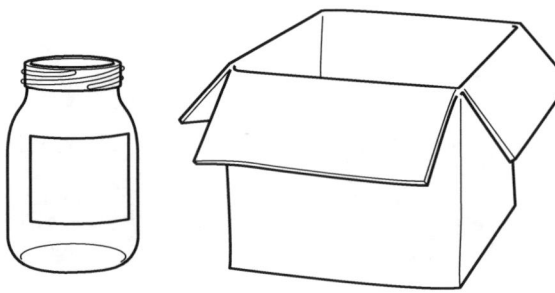

a jar   a big box

a spoon   a jar

a pan   a bucket

a bucket   a cup

Teacher's notes
Look at each pair of containers in turn. Colour the container that holds more in red and the container that holds less in green.

Name _____ Date _____

Sorting shoes

You need:
● scissors ● glue

● **Sort numbers using a diagram**

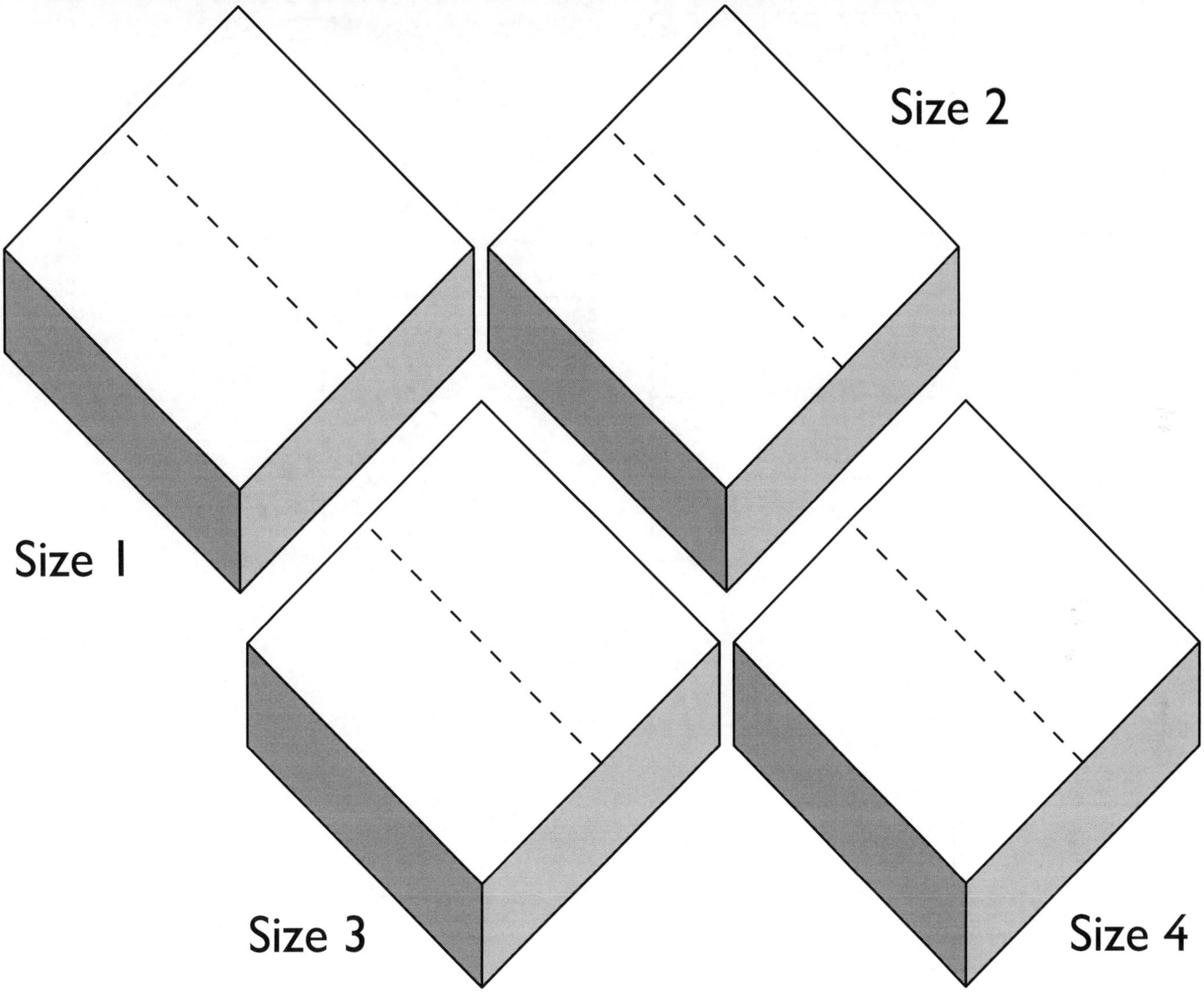

Size 2

Size 1

Size 3

Size 4

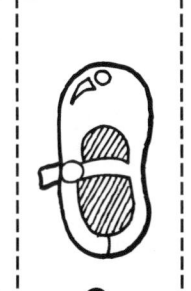
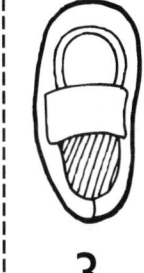

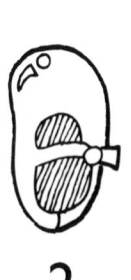
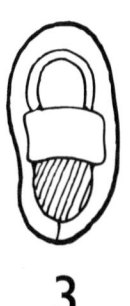

2   3   1   4   1   4   2   3

Teacher's notes
Cut out the shoes from the bottom of the sheet. Arrange them in pairs from smallest to largest. Stick them on the relevant boxes.

Name _____ Date _____

Recording the weather

You need:
● paper clip
● pencil

● **Record objects using a list**

	Draw shape here
1	
2	
3	
4	
5	
6	
7	
8	
9	
10	
11	
12	
13	
14	
15	

There are [ ] cloudy days.

There are [ ] rainy days.

There are [ ] sunny days.

Teacher's notes
Using the paper clip and pencil, spin the spinner and draw the picture you spin in the table.
Do this 15 times.

Name _____ Date _____

Thirsty work

You need:
● coloured pencils

● **Solve problems about capacity**

Jack drinks 2 glasses of orange juice.

| 3 | – | 2 | = | 1 |

Emily drinks 2 glasses of milk.

| ☐ | – | ☐ | = | ☐ |

Amisha drinks 1 glass of lemonade.

| 5 | – | ☐ | = | ☐ |

Her mum drinks 3 cups of tea.

| ☐ | – | ☐ | = | ☐ |

John drinks 4 glasses of water.

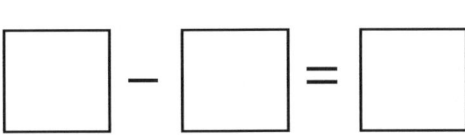

| ☐ | – | ☐ | = | ☐ |

Ravi drinks 2 mugs of coffee.

| ☐ | – | ☐ | = | ☐ |

Robert drinks 3 glasses of mango juice.

| ☐ | – | ☐ | = | ☐ |

Clare drinks 1 milkshake.

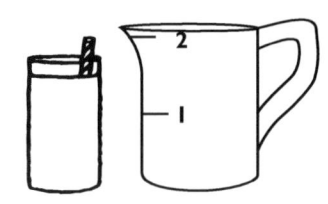

| ☐ | – | ☐ | = | ☐ |

Teacher's notes
Read the sentences to find out how many glasses have been poured from each full container. Work out how much will be left in the container. Then colour the liquid left and write the subtraction calculation.

Name _____ Date _____

Measuring juices

You need:
● coloured pencil

● **Display the capacity of a container with a scale**

4 cupfuls

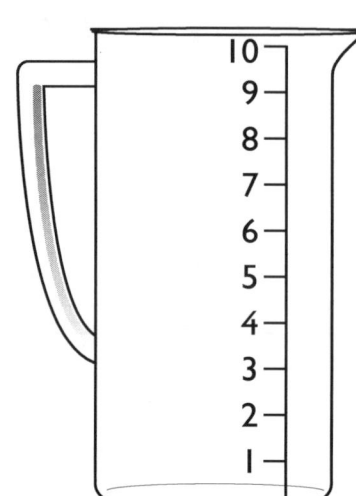

7 cupfuls

3 cupfuls

9 cupfuls

5 cupfuls

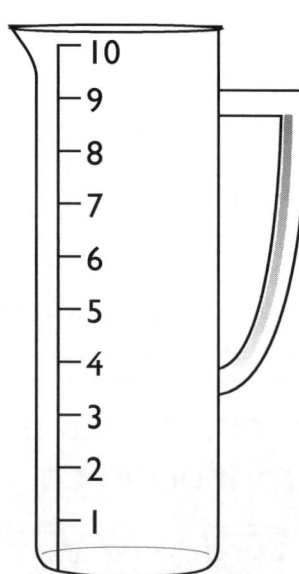

10 cupfuls

© HarperCollinsPublishers Ltd 2008

Teacher's notes
Each jug holds 10 cupfuls of juice. Look at the number of cupfuls that have been poured into each jug.
Draw a line and colour the juice to show how much is in each jug.

Name _____ Date _____

Name game

● **Sort objects using a diagram**

a b c d e f g h i j k l m n o p q r s t u v w x y z

e		t		i		a		o		n		s		h

Teacher's notes
Top section: In the left-hand boxes, write down the names of ten children in the class. In the right-hand boxes, rearrange the letters in each name in alphabetical order.
Bottom section: Count how many time each letter appears in all ten names. Complete the table.

Name _____ Date _____

Word length

You need:
● coloured pencil

● **Sort objects using diagrams**

5   3
these are the words to sort out

count the letters and write them in boxes

word length	number of words
2	
3	
4	
5	
6	
7	

Number of words

2	
3	
4	
5	
6	
7	

△ stands for one word

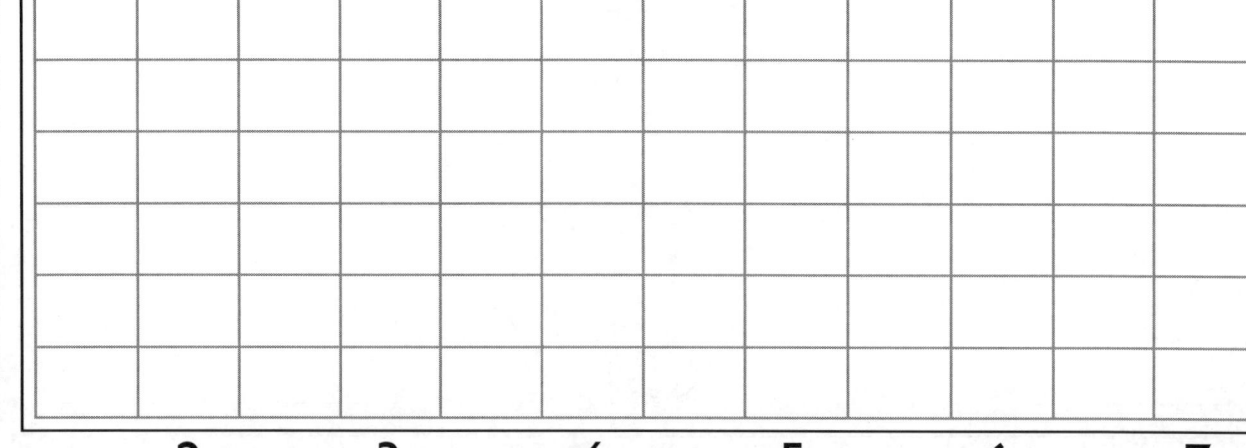

Number of words

2   3   4   5   6   7
word lengths

[ ] words have 5 letters.   There are no words with [ ] letters.

132

Teacher's notes
Count the letters in each word in the grey box and write the number of letters above each word. Complete the table. Then complete the pictogram and block graph. Then complete the sentences.

Name _____ Date _____

What's the time?

You need:
● scissors (per pair)

● **Use words about time**

one hour after	one hour before
half an hour after	half an hour before

✂

✂

Teacher's notes
Cut out the four instruction cards from the top panel and the six time cards from the bottom panel. Lay them out randomly in their two groups, printed side down. Taking turns, one person picks up one instruction card and one time card and reads out their messages in order. Another person gives the answer. Repeat.

Name _____ Date _____

Capacity problems

● **Measure the capacity of different containers**

Container A

holds ☐ cupfuls

Container B

holds ☐ cupfuls

Container C

holds ☐ cupfuls

Container D

holds ☐ cupfuls

Container ☐ holds the most.

Container ☐ holds the least.

You need:
● four different containers labelled A, B, C and D
● jug of water
● cup (per group)

Teacher's notes
Provide each group with the necessary resources. Children find the capacity of each container, writing their findings in the spaces provided.

Name _____ Date _____

Follow the directions!

You need:
● scissors ● glue

● Use words to describe position and direction

Put...

the football
| above |
the drum.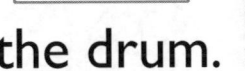

the robot
| below |
the train.

the car
on the | right | of
the elephant.

the kite
on the | left | of
the drum.

the doll
| between |
the kite
and the
elephant.

Choose a place for the teddy
and tell us where it is.

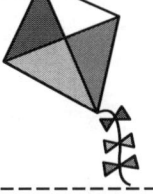

© HarperCollinsPublishers Ltd 2008

Teacher's notes
Cut out the pictures from the bottom of the sheet and follow the dsirections to put them into their correct positions on the grid.

135

Name _____ Date _____

Tens and twenties

You need:
● coloured pencil

● **Solve problems about money**

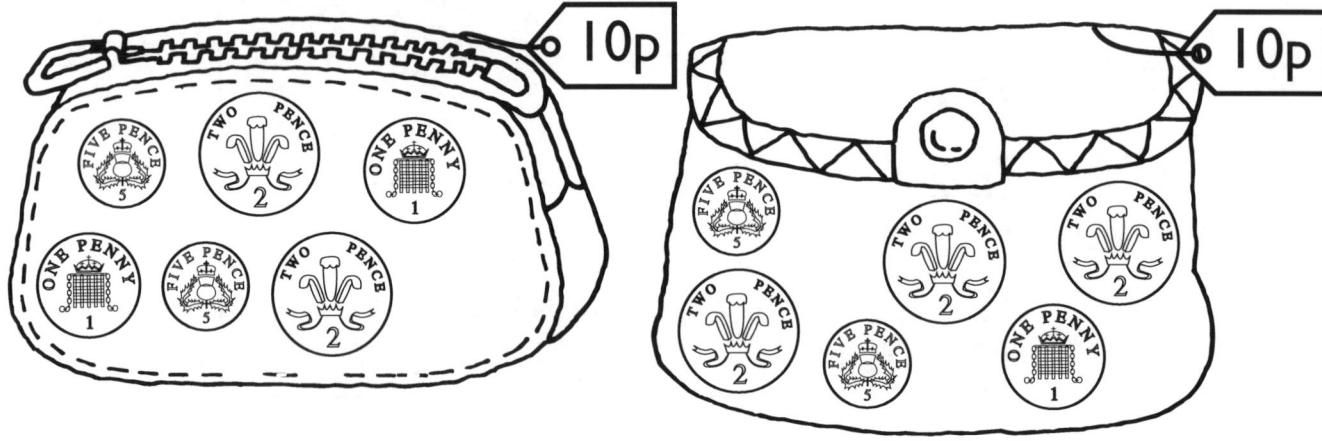

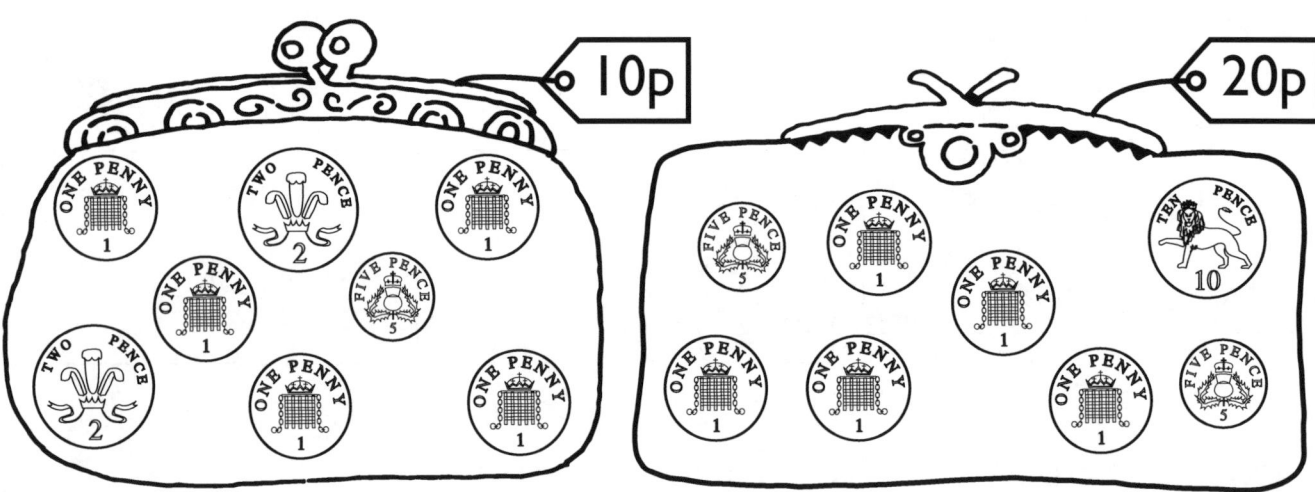

Teacher's notes
Look at the label on each purse. Colour the coins inside to show this amount, making sure that each combination of coins is different.

136

Name _____ Date _____

Hours and half hours

● **Use words related to time; read the time to the hour and half hour**

			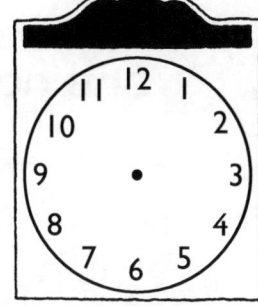
1 hour later	$\frac{1}{2}$ an hour later	1 hour before	$\frac{1}{2}$ an hour before
			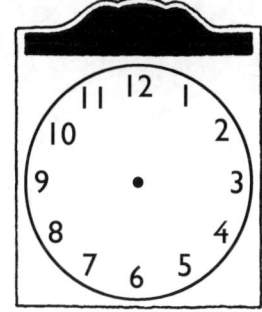
$\frac{1}{2}$ an hour before	1 hour before	$\frac{1}{2}$ an hour later	1 hour before

1 hour before	$\frac{1}{2}$ an hour before	1 hour later	1 hour later

© HarperCollinsPublishers Ltd 2008

Teacher's notes
Look at the time on each clock at the top of the sheet. Underneath, follow the instructions to show the correct time on each clock by drawing the hands on each clock face.

137

Name _____ Date _____

Earlier or later

● **Read the time to the hour and half hour**

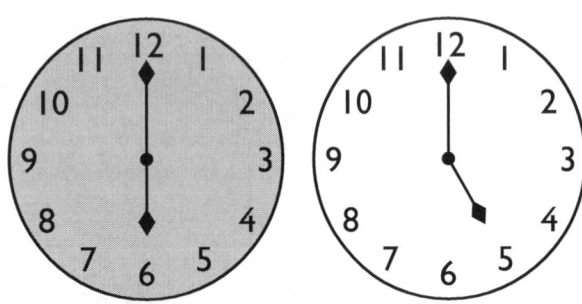

one hour earlier

one hour later

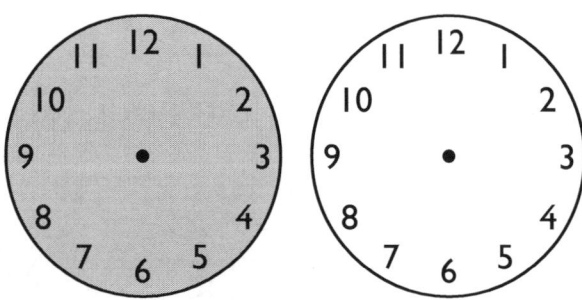

half hour earlier

4 hours later

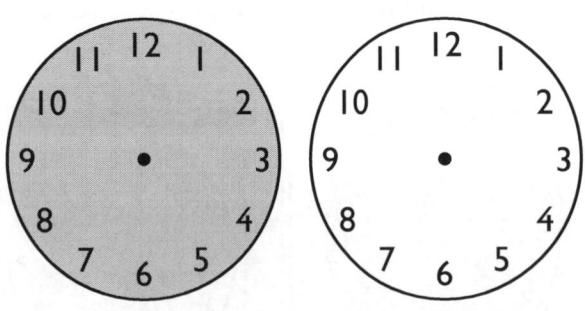

six hours earlier

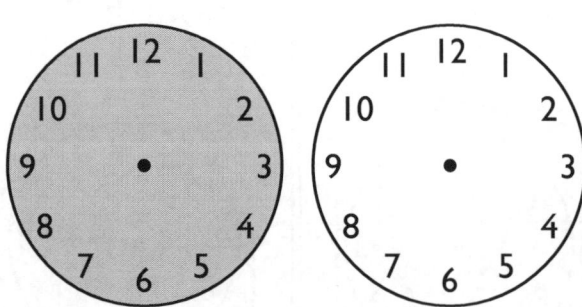

12 hours later

Teacher's notes

For each pair of clocks, first choose an o'clock or half past time and mark it on the left-hand
clock by drawing the two hands in their correct positions. Then, on the right-hand clock, mark
an earlier or later time as given. Use a different starting time for each pair of clocks.

Name _____ Date _____

Quarter turn squares

You need:
● scissors ● glue

● **Recognise quarter turns**

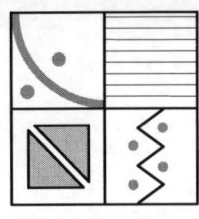   a quarter turn to the right   

   a quarter turn to the left   

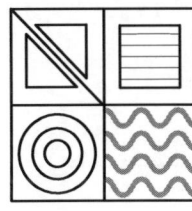   a quarter turn to the right   

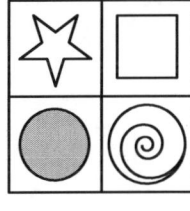   a quarter turn to the left   

   a quarter turn to the right   

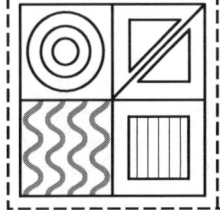 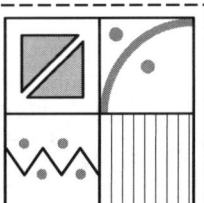 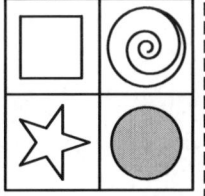  

Teacher's notes
Cut out each large square from the bottom of the sheet. Place each one on its matching square on the left, and follow the instructions, making a quarter turn to the right or left. Then glue the shape in the space provided to show its position after making the turn.

Name _____ Date _____

Money box savings

You need:
● scissors ● glue

● **Solve problems about money**

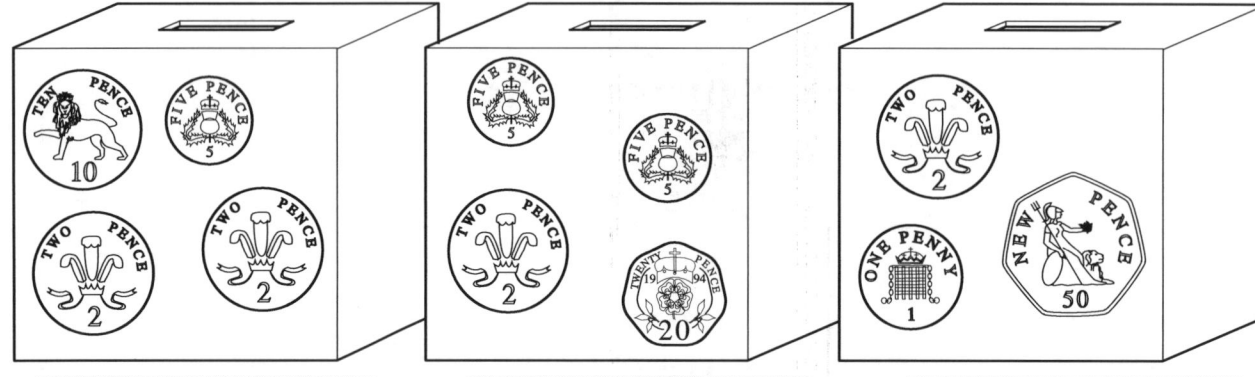

10p + 5p + 2p + 2p 10p + 5p + 4p 10p + 9p - 19p		

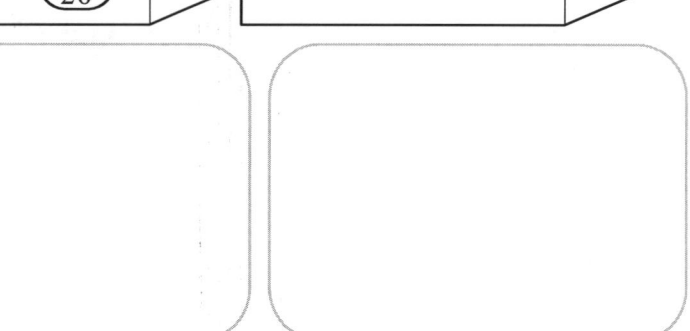

This moneybox has 25p

This moneybox has 30p

140

Teacher's notes

Top section: Work out how much is in each moneybox and show your addition calculation starting with the largest number first. *Bottom section:* Cut out the coins from the bottom of the sheet and work out which coins go into each money box.

Name _____ Date _____

1 whole, a half and a quarter

● **Understand whole, half and quarter**

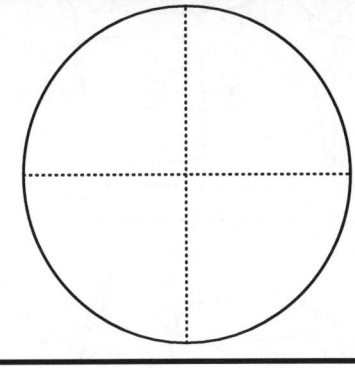 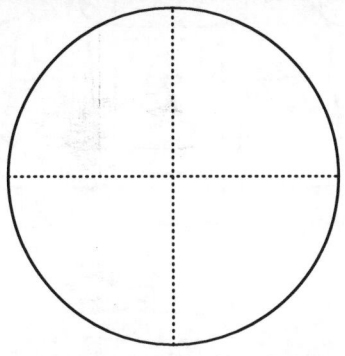 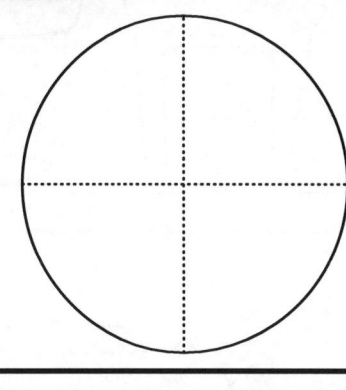

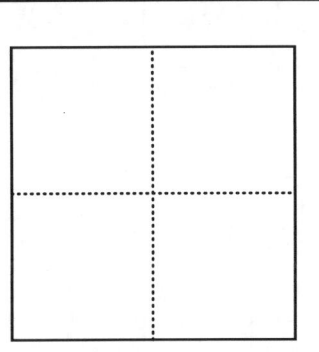 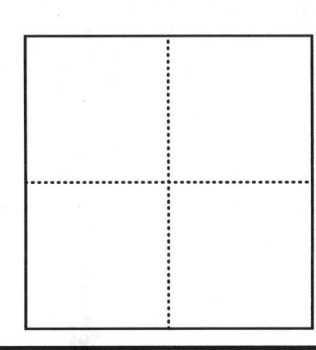 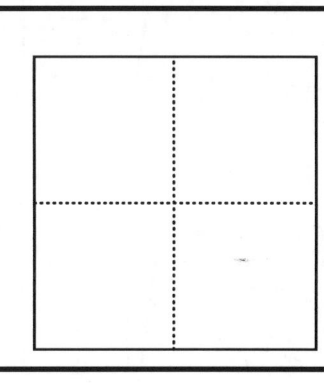

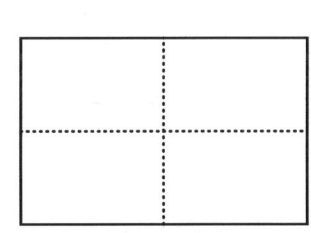 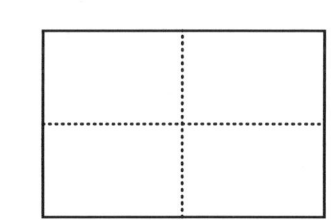

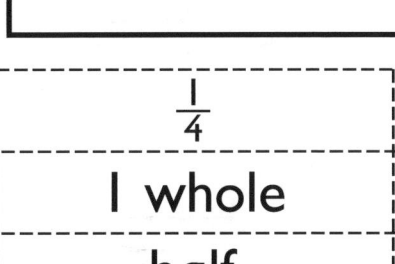

I whole	$\frac{1}{4}$	$\frac{1}{4}$
half	I whole	$\frac{1}{2}$
quarter	half	I whole

Teacher's notes
In each row, shade each shape to show 1 whole, a quarter and a half. Cut out the labels at the bottom of the sheet and stick them in the correct spaces underneath each shape.

Name _____ Date _____

Plenty of pots

● Choose two numbers to make a given total

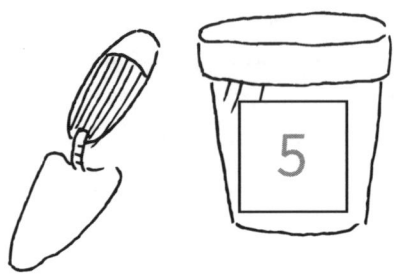 5 + 6 = 11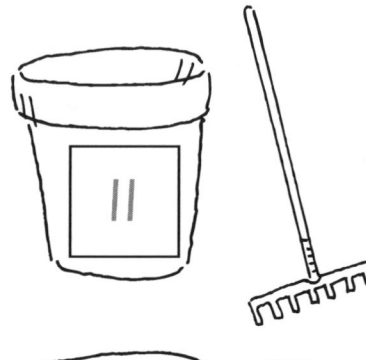

 ☐ + ☐ = 12

 ☐ + ☐ = 13

 ☐ + ☐ = 14

Teacher's notes
Look at the numbers on the pots on the shelf.
Refer to these numbers to write the appropriate number on each pair of
pots and solve the resulting addition calculation.

Name _____ Date _____

Counting caterpillars

● **Count on or back in twos, fives and tens**

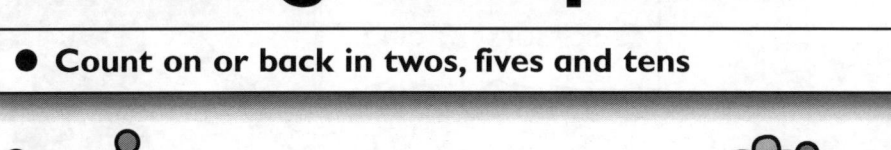

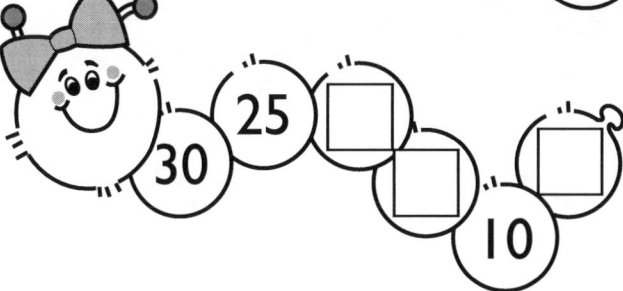
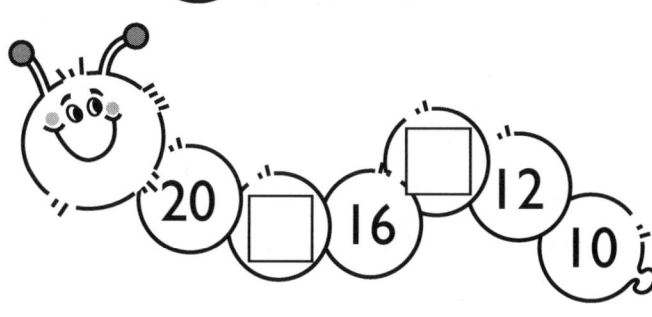

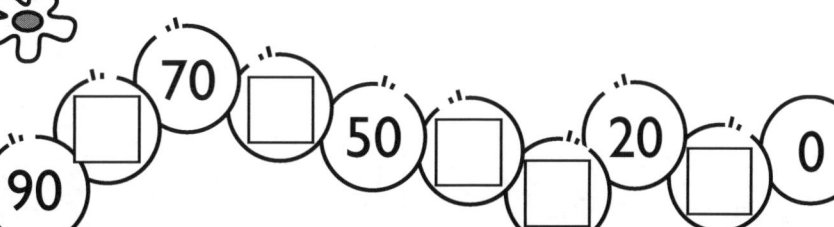

Teacher's notes
Look at the number sequences on each caterpillar. In each sequence, count on or back in 2s, 5s or 10s to find and write the missing numbers.

143

Name _____   Date _____

Dinosaur
tracks of twos

You need:
- ● scissors ● glue

- ● **Count on in twos**

---

0   4   8   [ ]

2   [6]   [ ]

---

1   [ ]   [ ]   [ ]

3   7   11

---

12   [ ]   20   [ ]

14   18   [ ]

---

13   [ ]   21   [ ]

15   19   [ ]

---

23   25   12   16   24   13

6   9   22   10   5   17

Teacher's notes
Cut out the pictures of the footprints from the bottom of the sheet. Then, in each
sequence of footprints, count on in twos to find the missing numbers, putting in the
appropriate pictures to complete the sequence.

Name _____ Date _____

Sets of socks

You need:
● scissors ● glue

● Solve problems combining groups of 2

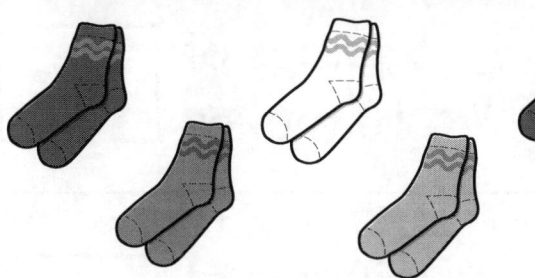

(5) pairs have ☐ socks

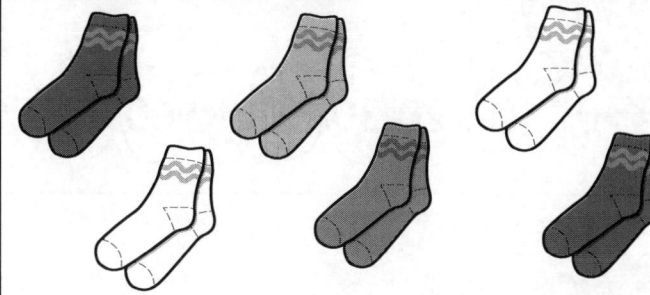

( ) pairs have ☐ socks

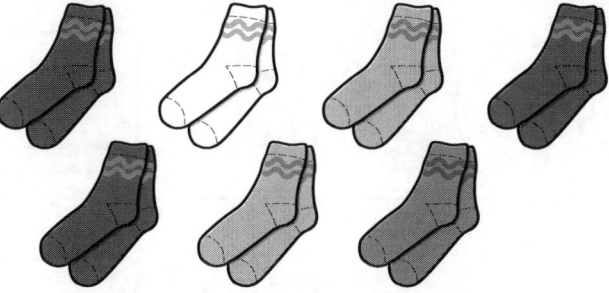

( ) pairs have ☐ socks

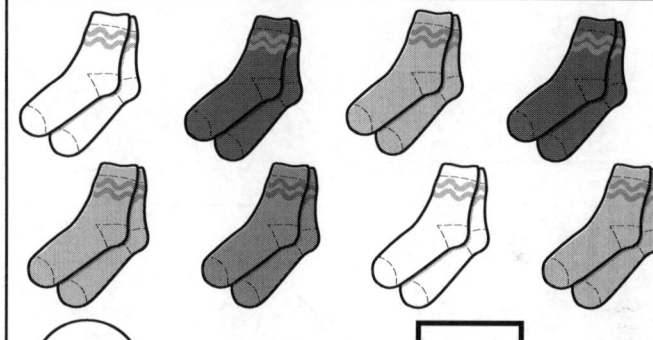
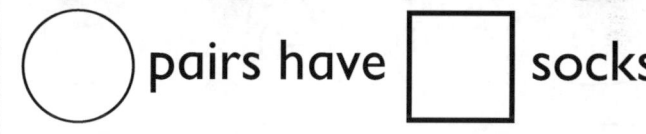

( ) pairs have ☐ socks

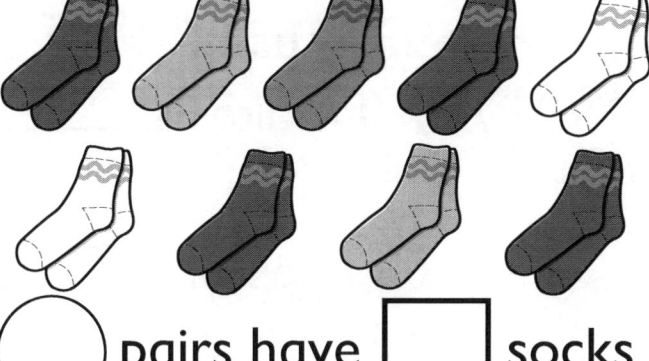

( ) pairs have ☐ socks

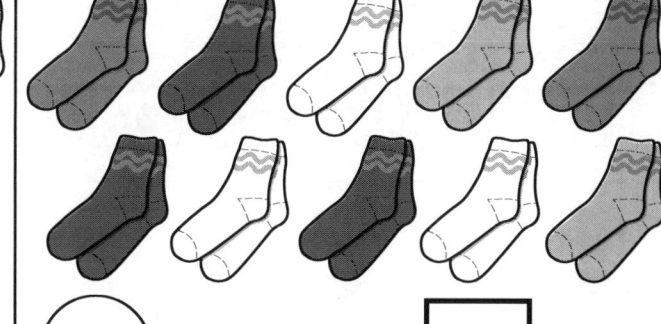

( ) pairs have ☐ socks

| 16 | 12 | 18 | 10 | 20 | 14 |

Teacher's notes
Cut out the multiples of two from the bottom of the sheet. Complete each statement
correctly by sticking the appropriate number next to each.

© HarperCollinsPublishers Ltd 2008

Name _____ Date _____

Tens totals

You need:
- scissors
- glue

- **Solve problems combining groups of 10**

5 jumps of 10 makes [ ]

6 jumps of 10 makes [ ]

7 jumps of 10 makes [ ]

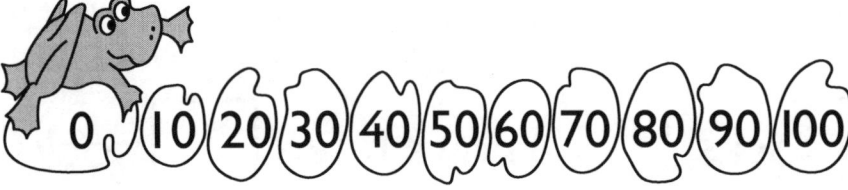

8 jumps of 10 makes [ ]

9 jumps of 10 makes [ ]

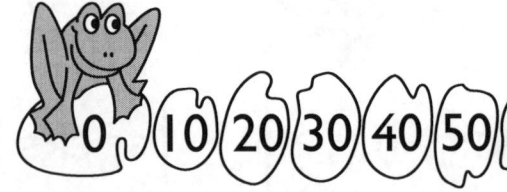

10 jumps of 10 makes [ ]

| 80 | 70 | 50 | 90 | 60 | 100 |  |

Teacher's notes
The frog makes jumps of 10 over the lily pads. Use the tens number track to work out how many lily pads she jumps over altogether. Show the jumps on the track, then cut out the correct answer and stick it in the space provided.

Name _____ Date _____

Half and quarter constellations

You need:
● scissors ● glue
● coloured pencils

● Find half and quarter of groups of objects

| $\frac{1}{4}$ of 12 | $\frac{1}{2}$ of 10 | half of 14 | $\frac{1}{4}$ of 20 | quarter of 8 | $\frac{1}{2}$ of 18 |

Teacher's notes
Look at each group of stars and the calculations in the bottom section. Count the total number of stars in each group to find which calculation should be glued underneath. Work out each calculation and colour the correct number of stars to show the answer.

Name _____ Date _____

Ten pin bowling

You need:
● scissors ● glue

● **Solve number puzzles**

Mia scores …

☐	+ ☐	+ ☐	=	☐

Amir scores …

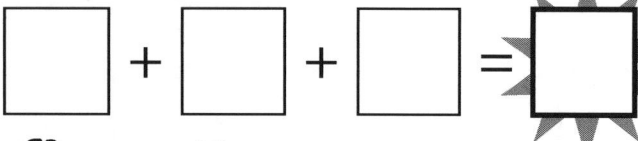

☐	+ ☐	+ ☐	=	☐

Ellie scores …

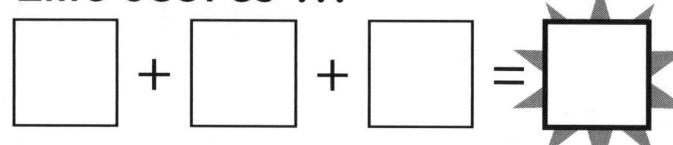

☐	+ ☐	+ ☐	=	☐

Theo scores …

☐	+ ☐	+ ☐	=	☐

Stripes' total score				Spots' total score		
☐	+ ☐	= ☐		☐	+ ☐	= ☐

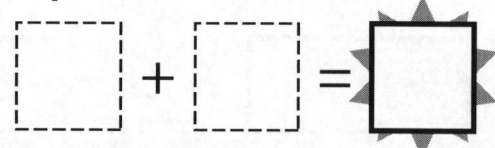

12	21	11	13	10	25	✂

© HarperCollins Publishers Ltd 2008

Teacher's notes

Top section: Work out each player's score by writing in the boxes the numbers on the three skittles and then adding them up. *Bottom section:* Cut out the numbers and stick in the scores of the two players in the Striped T-shirt. Add them to get the stripes total score. Repeat for the Spots.

Name _____ Date _____

Planets Odd and Even

You need:
● scissors ● glue

● **Recognise odd and even numbers to 30**

Planet Even

Planet Odd

| 28 | 20 | 7 | 19 | 16 | 25 |
| 13 | 24 | 11 | 12 | 15 | 10 |

Teacher's notes

Cut out the pictures of the monsters at the bottom of the sheet. Look at the number on each monster, decide whether it is odd or even and then stick it on the correct planet.

Name _____ Date _____

Multiple madness!

You need:
- red, yellow and blue coloured pencils

● Recognise multiples of 2, 5 and 10

18 35 12 5

 20 45 25 90

8 100 35

40 18

4

60

30

6

15 14

50 70

2 80 10 16

150

Teacher's notes
Look at each number and decide whether it is a multiple of 2, 5 or 10. If it is a multiple of 2, circle it in red; a multiple of 5, circle it in yellow and a multiple of 10 in blue. Are there any numbers circled more than once? Which ones are they?

Name _____ Date _____

Five penny purses

You need:
● scissors ● glue

● **Solve problems combining groups of 5**

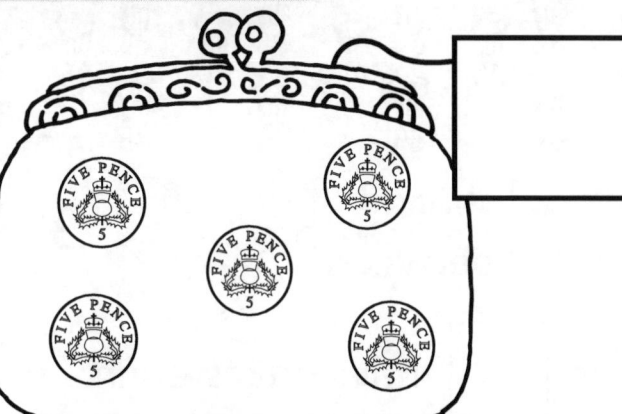

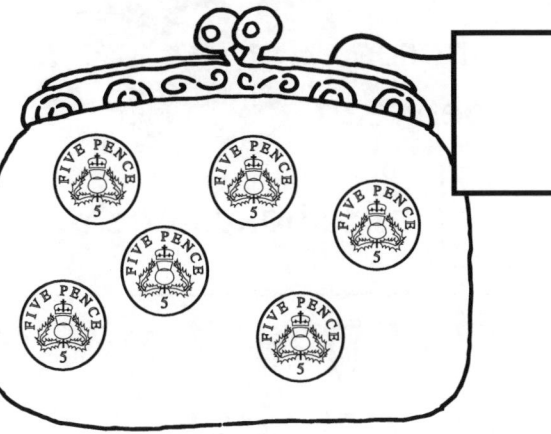

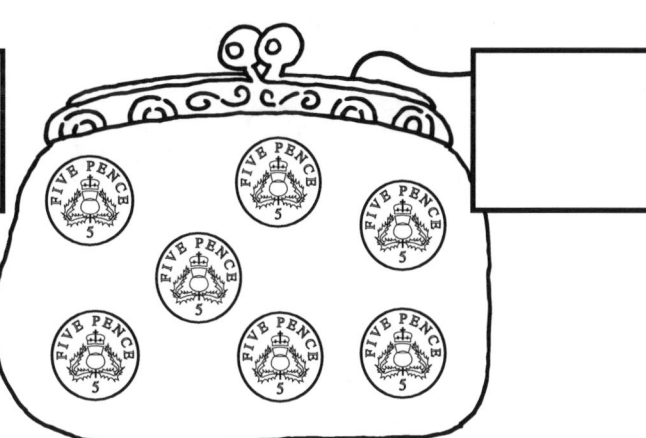

| 35p | 50p | 30p | 45p | 25p | 40p |

Teacher's notes
Cut out the answers from the bottom of the sheet. Look at the 5p coins in each purse.
Calculate the total amount in each one and stick the correct answer on to the label of
each purse.

© HarperCollinsPublishers Ltd 2008

Name _____ Date _____

Milkshake shares

● **Solve problems involving sharing into equal groups**

| 12 | shared between |  3 |

is [ ] milkshakes each.

[ ] shared between  4

is [ ] milkshakes each.

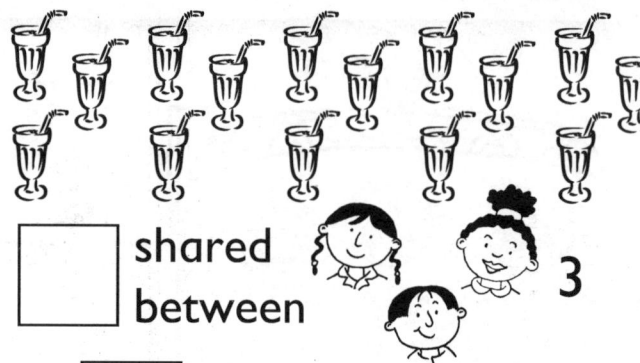

[ ] shared between 3

is [ ] milkshakes each.

[ ] shared between  5

is [ ] milkshakes each.

[ ] shared between  2

is [ ] milkshakes each.

[ ] shared between  2

is [ ] milkshakes each.

[ ] shared between  4

is [ ] milkshakes each.

[ ] shared between  5

is [ ] milkshakes each.

Teacher's notes
Share the milkshakes between two, three, four or five children,
writing the answers in the spaces provided.